Student's Transcript of
GREGG
SHORTHAND
FOR COLLEGES
Volume Two
Diamond Jubilee Series
Second Edition

Louis A. Leslie
Coauthor Diamond Jubilee Series of Gregg Shorthand

Charles E. Zoubek
Coauthor Diamond Jubilee Series of Gregg Shorthand

A. James Lemaster
Editor in Chief, Gregg Shorthand

Russell J. Hosler
Professor Emeritus, University of Wisconsin

Gregg Division|McGraw-Hill Book Company
New York|St. Louis|Dallas|San Francisco
Auckland|Düsseldorf|Johannesburg|Kuala Lumpur
London|Mexico|Montreal|New Delhi|Panama|Paris
São Paulo|Singapore|Sydney|Tokyo|Toronto

Student's Transcript of
GREGG
SHORTHAND
FOR
COLLEGES,
Diamond Jubilee Series,
Volume Two,
Second Edition

7 8 9 0 WCWC 2 1 0 9

ISBN 07-037407-4

Explanation to Users of This Booklet

This booklet contains the transcript to the shorthand material in the Reading and Writing Practice exercises of *Gregg Shorthand for Colleges, Diamond Jubilee Series, Volume Two,* Second Edition. The number preceding each exercise corresponds to the shorthand exercise number in the text, *Gregg Shorthand for Colleges, Diamond Jubilee Series, Volume Two.* This transcript will serve two desirable purposes:

1 It will enable the student to look up the word or phrase represented by any outline about which he is in doubt. He will thus be able to cover the Reading and Writing Practice exercises more quickly and with a minimum of discouragement.

2 Because the key material is counted, the student will be able to obtain extra dictation practice outside of class.

The Publishers

Transcript of Shorthand

(The material is counted in groups of 20 standard words or 28 syllables for convenience in timing the reading or dictation.)

Chapter 1

LESSON 1

3 Dear Mr. Best: It was a pleasure meeting you last week to discuss the possibility of your joining our[1] organization in a position in the accounting department. We were particularly impressed with[2] your educational background, training, and experience.

Consequently, we are offering you a position[3] starting Tuesday, January 2, at a salary of $10,000 a year. If this is[4] satisfactory to you, Mr. Best, please let us have your confirmation by return mail.

You will find that working[5] in our company is both interesting and challenging. You will have, in addition, an opportunity[6] to advance rapidly. Sincerely yours,   [127]

4 Dear Mr. Long: Thank you, Mr. Long, for your letter offering me a position in your accounting department.[1] I am delighted to accept. The type of work required by your organization is the kind I enjoy[2] most.

The salary of $10,000 a year is satisfactory. I am happy to know, however,[3] that the opportunities for advancement are good. You will find me to be a dependable, loyal worker,[4] and I am eager to prove myself to you. I look forward to joining your staff on January 2. Very[5] truly yours,   [102]

5 Dear Mr. Smith: Haven't we met before? Most people get acquainted with the Royal Supper Club by going as[1] the guest of a member.

Perhaps you have been a guest recently and have wished that you were also a member[2] of our club. We would like to extend to you a special invitation to become a member of the Royal Supper[3] Club yourself. For a short time we are offering a limited number of memberships at a special[4] initial charge of $25, which is only half the regular fee.

We think that you would enjoy being[5] a member of one of the most beautiful clubs in Detroit. Your membership provides you with an exclusive place[6] to which you can take clients, friends, or even your boss! The special membership gives you your own key with full club[7] privileges.

The enclosed brochure tells the complete Royal Supper Club story. Return the application and get ready[8] for our own special brand of hospitality. Sincerely yours,   [173]

6 Dear Mrs. Kingston: Thank you for your order for doubleknit cloth. Unfortunately, we are temporarily[1] out of stock of this item. However, we expect another shipment in August, and we will fill your order[2] when our stock arrives.

In the meantime, Mrs. Kingston, won't you look through the enclosed catalog. In it you will find[3] many new designs and patterns that I am sure you will want to use in your new fall wardrobe. Sincerely yours,[4] [80]

7 Dear Mr. Hayes: We are delighted to hear that you are considering studying in England this summer.

Enclosed[1] is the list of the schools in England that offer programs of summer study that will be of interest to[2] you. As you requested, we are sending you an itinerary of the sight-seeing trip that is sponsored by[3] our travel agency.

We are sure, Mr. Hayes, that if you decide to study in England, you will have one[4] of the most enjoyable summers ever. Yours very truly, [91]

8 Dear Mrs. Thomas: It was indeed a pleasure to receive your letter of February 12. We were concerned[1] about your not having paid your bills for the months of November, December, and January, but we knew that[2] there must have been a good reason.

Won't you come in to our office on Friday, March 3, at 2 p.m., at which time[3] we can work out a special plan that will enable you to pay your bills over an extended period of[4] time.

We value you as a customer and want to continue our business relationship for many years[5] to come. Cordially yours, [104]

9 Dear Mrs. Peterson: There are some things a woman cannot ask a man. Who should know this better than another[1] woman? That is why the State Realty Company has appointed Miss Mary Johnson as a special consultant[2] to women who face the problems of moving from one home to another.

Miss Johnson can give you tips on selling[3] your house, on the best way to transport the family dog, or on how to pack a special item so that it will[4] arrive in good condition.

Miss Johnson can provide up-to-date facts about schools, churches, and shopping centers for the[5] woman who is wondering about her new hometown. This service is free through the State Realty Company.[6]

Won't you give Miss Johnson the opportunity to help you in a personal way the next time you plan to move.[7] Sincerely yours, [142]

LESSON 2

14 Dear Mr. Fox: As you know, we are interested in buying the timber rights on your land near Seattle,[1] Washington. We would agree, of course, to your stipulation that we take only half the timber in each area[2] and replant where we cut the trees.

Would it be possible for you to discuss specific arrangements with me sometime[3] next week? I am free every day except Thursday. Please let me know the day and time that will be most convenient[4] for you. Sincerely yours, [84]

15 Dear Mr. Malone: During the past year there was a severe water shortage in many states. Yet damaging floods[1] cost Americans millions of dollars during the same year. Too much water and too little water are

really[2] different sides of the same problem. The problem is poor water management.

In droughts there is no reserve water[3] available, and floods occur when proper controls are lacking. Good water management includes saving in[4] times of plenty for use in times of need.

As our nation grows and as our world grows, our water needs will also grow.[5] It is important, therefore, to get every drop of use out of every drop of water.

For help in getting[6] your community started on a water management program, write for the free booklet, *Our Water Crisis*. We[7] will be happy to send it to you if you will sign and return the enclosed stamped, addressed card. Sincerely yours,[8] [160]

16 Dear Mr. Johnson: Ecology is everybody's business. It is not just the concern of the company[1] with the big smokestack or the one polluting the stream. Everybody must accept the responsibility[2] of keeping our country beautiful and of conserving our natural resources.

If you are interested[3] in joining a local group devoted to protecting the environment, join us in an organizational[4] meeting on Friday, June 15. Full details are given in the enclosed folder.

Remember, Mr. Johnson,[5] ecology is everybody's business. Very truly yours, [113]

17 Dear Miss Weber: We think you have made a wise choice in de-ciding to further your education by attending[1] college. More jobs will be open to you when you graduate, and you will be able to earn a higher salary.[2]

After reviewing your high school records, Miss Weber, we find that you are eligible to apply for[3] several scholarships here at Connecticut State College. Enclosed are the application forms for these scholarships.[4] We are also sending you our general catalog. Very sincerely yours, [94]

18 Dear Professor Smith: Your letter indicating that you were recommending me for a position on your science[1] staff was certainly good news. I have long admired the program that you have in science at Los Angeles[2] University, and being a member of the faculty would be stimulating, interesting, and challenging.[3]

You indicated that before the administration can take action, it will be necessary for me[4] to come to the campus to meet with the dean of the School of Liberal Arts and the vice president in charge of[5] academic affairs. I could be on campus all day Wednesday, April 7. Will you please let me know if this[6] is convenient for you. Cordially yours, [127]

19 Dear Mr. James: Next fall our company will be enlarging its home office by adding two floors, and we would like[1] to have you help us. The new space will be used to house our central files for our five branch offices. We hope to use[2] open-shelf filing because we understand that it is convenient, inexpensive, and economical to[3] operate.

We are now facing the problems of designing the new area to make the best use of the[4] open-shelf filing system. Do you suggest some special support for the floors? What kind of fireproofing is necessary[5] for this type of filing system? Do you have additional suggestions that can help us?

I would appreciate[6] it, Mr. James, if you could arrange to have a representative visit our office on Friday, June[7] 12, to discuss our problems with us. Sincerely yours,   [150]

LESSON 3

23 Dear Mrs. Black: You will recall that when you placed your order with us two weeks ago for one of our gas ranges,[1] we promised you delivery by the end of December. I regret to advise you, Mrs. Black, that we will[2] not be able to keep our promise.

We have just received word from the manufacturer that because of a fire[3] in his plant last month, all production of gas ranges has been stopped. The company expects to resume operations[4] in a few days, and we should have your range in our store by January 15. As soon as we receive it,[5] we will deliver it to you.

We apologize for any inconvenience this delay in delivery[6] may cause you. Yours very truly,   [126]

24 Dear Mrs. Strong: It is amazing but true! Our new electronic range cooks your food for any meal in just minutes.[1] It is the fastest, most efficient method of cooking ever devised. Just plug the oven into any[2] outlet and turn it on. Simple, isn't it? The food gets hot, but the oven stays cool.

Your food is cooked more evenly[3] than ever before and retains its natural juices.

For more information about our electronic[4] range, Mrs. Strong, see your General dealer today. He will be glad to give you a demonstration and a free[5] booklet describing sample meals that can be cooked in our range in less than 15 minutes. Sincerely yours,   [119]

25 Dear Mr. Mitchell: It will be a pleasure for our organization, The Homemakers' Club, to participate[1] in your campaign to raise money for the Cancer Research Fund.

We have already started selling tickets for the[2] dinner on March 19. At our meeting last night eight people indicated that they would attend. Many of our[3] members were out of town yesterday, and we would like to offer the tickets for sale again at our next meeting[4] on Tuesday, March 11. Therefore, we will not be able to let you know definitely until March 12 how[5] many people will attend. Sincerely yours,   [108]

26 Dear Mr. O'Brien: Is your company drowning in a sea of paper work? Is the "information explosion"[1] creating more facts, figures, and reports than you can possibly handle or analyze? If your office has become[2] a victim of increased paper work and the accompanying increased expenses, you will be glad

to hear[3] about our new computer service.

The Royal Computer Company can cut your paper work and clerical[4] expenses substantially and, at the same time, give you more pertinent information. The Royal Company[5] can install in your office a computer terminal connected by local telephone wires to our main[6] computer many miles away. When you need information, you simply type a request and you have your answer within[7] a matter of seconds. Gone is the need for long hours at the calculator. Gone are the worries about[8] mathematical mistakes. But, best of all, gone are many of your clerical expenses.

When you rent a computer[9] terminal from us, you pay a low monthly rental fee plus a service charge for the time you use the computer.[10] You never have to pay for the computer itself.

Let one of our representatives demonstrate how you[11] can take advantage of the "information explosion" without being buried by it. Sincerely yours, [239]

27 Dear Mr. Henderson: It is my duty, as mayor of Springfield, to do everything possible to promote[1] the employment opportunities of our city. It is in the light of this responsibility that[2] I write concerning a matter that has recently caused much concern in Springfield.

There is a rumor that your factory[3] will close for the entire month of December to modernize its facilities and that all your employees[4] will be without work during this critical month.

I realize that you must modernize your equipment, but[5] I hope that you can arrange a modernization program that will not necessitate a complete shutdown of[6] your factory.

I am sure that you are sensitive to the concern that I express, and I hope that we can reassure[7] the people of our community that the rumor is false. Sincerely yours, [154]

LESSON 4

31 Dear Mr. Wilson: If you are like most men, you do not enjoy repairing small appliances at home. Many[1] essentially good appliances are thrown away every year because they do not work properly, and the[2] cost of having them fixed is prohibitive.

The reason most people do not like to repair small appliances[3] is that they do not understand how the appliances operate. That is why we have just purchased several[4] thousand copies of a new book for our customers. It is called *Appliance Repairs Made Easy,* and it explains[5] simply and briefly how to repair most of the small appliances in your home. It specifies the tools needed[6] and gives tips on how to avoid problems.

We have a free copy of the book reserved for you at our hardware store.[7] Drop in the next time you are in the neighborhood, Mr. Wilson, and pick it up. No purchase is necessary.[8] Cordially yours, [162]

32 Dear Mr. Gibbs: When your wife asks, "Can you fix it, Dear?"

answer her with a gun—the Gaines Staple Gun! This handy staple[1] gun should be a basic tool in every home. It helps you install carpets, put fabric on walls, and do[2] 101 other things around the house.

This stapler has lots of power for those extra-hard surfaces. Yet,[3] it installs staples without damaging the adjacent area. It also has a built-in extractor. Best[4] of all, the stapler costs only $11. To order your stapler, just fill in, sign, and return the enclosed[5] order blank. Send for your staple gun today. It is so easy to use that your wife can do the job herself![6] Sincerely yours,   [122]

33 Dear Mr. Kelly: Thank you for your letter requesting further information about our correspondence courses[1] in reading. We have ten different courses that range from basic reading to advanced speed reading.

Each course contains[2] 20 lessons. These lessons consist of text material, problems, and exercises that you complete and return[3] to your correspondence instructor.

Our complete catalog is enclosed. Sincerely yours,   [77]

34 Dear Mr. Abbot: If you value your trees, have the Johnson Tree Service inspect them. Well-cared-for trees, with their cool[1] shade and changing colors, help make a house a beautiful home.

Healthy trees can greatly enhance the value of your[2] property. That is why it is wise to have a Johnson representative inspect all your trees thoroughly.

The[3] Johnson man will suggest a program to keep your valuable trees healthy. With his experience and training,[4] he can determine precisely what your trees need.

Call your local Johnson representative today to arrange for[5] an inspection and maintenance program for your trees. Entrust your trees to Johnson; they will be in good hands! Yours very[6] truly,   [121]

35 Dear Mr. Barnes: Early this year we introduced the National electric shaver. If you have not yet seen it,[1] come into our store soon for a demonstration. The National gives the closest, fastest shave ever. In trial[2] tests, 95 percent of the men using the National shaver said that it shaved closer than a blade.

The[3] National gives you a much more comfortable shave than any other electric shaver on the market. The secret[4] is in the shaving heads. They gently press down the skin around each whisker and allow the blades to cut at the[5] skin level.

The National gives you a unique shave, a shave that is close but still comfortable. See the new[6] National electric shaver today. You will be glad you did. Sincerely yours, [134]

36 Dear Mr. Green: Christmas is just around the corner, and we want to be one of the first to wish you a delightful[1] holiday season.

This year we have some suggestions to help you enjoy Christmas more. In the enclosed folder[2] we have described two things to take some of the unnecessary hustle and bustle out of your life.

1. A simple[3] way to have your

Christmas stamps delivered to your home.

2. Unusual gift ideas you can order by[4] mail for the people on your list who are stamp collectors.

Another helpful suggestion we would like to make is[5] this: Mail early.

All the employees of your local post office wish you the happiest of Christmases. Cordially[6] yours, [121]

37 Dear Mr. Stone: Thank you for your letter indicating that your client, Mr. Harry C. Robin, is selling[1] his residence on Lake George.

My family and I have been looking for the past several months for a large home on[2] a lake with a private beach. We have not found anything thus far that meets our specifications.

The description[3] you gave of this property, however, indicates that it is just about the size and type of property that[4] we would like.

I will be extremely busy during the next two weeks and will not be free to go to Lake George until[5] the week of June 10. Could you arrange for me to see the house on Monday, June 11, or Tuesday, June 12?[6] Sincerely yours, [122]

LESSON 5

40 *The History of Pens*

Most people during the Dark Ages could neither read nor write, and those few who could wrote crudely. Priests and monks made gallant[1] efforts to uphold culture. They gave posterity beautifully decorated letter forms, the custom[2] of paragraphing and margining, and the first efforts at punctuation.

The documents which have been handed[3] down from the seventh through the tenth centuries, including bills, charters, and wills, were written with India ink. This[4] innovation was an important step forward because the inks used retained their color to a greater degree[5] than those of preceding periods.

Another bright point in the history of inks and pens during this period[6] was the invention of the quill pen sometime during the sixth century. It permitted a degree of latitude[7] in writing never before known, for the inks were a great deal thinner than before.

The quill, so widely used[8] until the advent of the metal pen, was adopted as early as the sixth century. Thus for over a[9] thousand years the quill was the writing instrument of the civilized western world.

Quill pens were never a really[10] practical writing tool. Not only did quill pens wear out quickly, but they also had other disadvantages.[11] Before the era of paper, when parchment and skin were used, an amazing amount of writing equipment[12] and preparation were necessary before a quill pen writer could make use of one of these instruments.

The[13] quill has played important roles in literature and history. It was with a quill pen that King John of England[14] signed the Magna Charta, and it was with the same kind of instrument that the Declaration of Independence[15] was signed.

With his new-found writing instruments, especially the quill and better inks, man's handwriting began[16] to change. He had written in block letters until scholars, around the twelfth century, began to use a form of[17] writing similar to longhand.

Capitals took on forms as we now know them. Small letters assumed a slant and[18] occasionally connecting strokes. Gradually writers turned to a form of making letters that was less stiff and[19] more suitable to speed so that they could make their writing instruments slide along with their thoughts.

Once man had evolved[20] an easier form of handwriting and had developed better inks which flowed readily from the pen, he again[21] set out in search of a better writing instrument.

Although it might have seemed a logical development, the[22] steel pen did not come from the quill. There were intermediate stages in the years between 1800 and[23] 1835. During that time there was a great search for substitutes for the quill. It is recorded that steel pens[24] were made in England as early as 1780, but it was not until some years later that steel pens won[25] any great acceptance.

These early steel pens were soon improved upon. They were made by punching a rough blank out of[26] steel, rounding it into a barrel shape, and marking a place for a slit with a sharp chisel. Before tempering,[27] the pen was tapped carefully with a small hammer to crack it.

In 1803 a man from Pennsylvania[28] took out the first fountain pen patent, but it was not until the 1880's that the fountain pen became[29] a practical writing instrument. Even these pens were not widely used, and as recently as 1900[30] very few people in the United States used fountain pens.

Early fountain pens consisted of a barrel into[31] which was fitted a point, often made of gold. One type of pen was designed to use steel points which could, if necessary,[32] be replaced. Besides the pen and barrel there was a feed bar under the pen to hold the ink as it was[33] supplied from the barrel. The principle governing the feed was based on gravity.

From the early 1900's[34] to the present day, vast improvements in pens have been realized, and the pen industry has grown by leaps and[35] bounds.

Today there are more than 130 American companies engaged in the manufacture of[36] pens or pen parts, and it has been estimated that about 75 percent of the world's pens are made in[37] America or by American subsidiaries located overseas. [755]— Adapted from *The History of Writing,* distributed by the Parker Pen Company.

Chapter 2

LESSON 6

43 Dear Mr. Jennings: If you want to get the most for your money, you should always shop in a Worth Department Store.¹ We have been in business for over 30 years, and we have the largest selection of merchandise in the state.²

Our success has been the result in part of good retailing practices, but the major part of our success³ comes from the loyal customers who have made Worth stores the most popular in the state.

Whether you need clothing,⁴ furniture, or general merchandise, visit our main store on Elm Street or any one of our branches throughout the⁵ city. Get your money's worth—the Worth way. Sincerely yours,   [110]

44 Dear Mr. White: As everyone knows, hotels and swimming pools all over the world are pretty much the same.

When¹ you plan a vacation in a foreign country, the factor that will make your trip particularly worthwhile is² what you see and do outside the hotel.

The Dunlap Travel Agency has been helping travelers see the world³ for years. We plan trips that are real experiences, not just hotel visits.

This year Dunlap has added a⁴ new service. You can now rent one of our cars for five days or more for a flat rate in the United States and Europe.⁵ In fact, you can rent a car from Dunlap almost anywhere in the world and drive all the miles you

want for only⁶ a reasonable daily charge. There is no mileage fee.

Won't you call us for more information or stop in⁷ to see us soon. Sincerely yours,   [146]

45 Dear Mrs. Gray: Perhaps you, like many other homeowners, have installed wood paneling in your house. If you have¹ paneled rooms, are they as attractive as you would like? Perhaps the wood does not look as nice as your table tops, your² piano, or your desk. If the paneling looks dull, everything else looks dull, too.

Panel Magic is a clear³ polish that is especially made to clean wood paneling and to leave it not only glowing but also protected⁴ from the drying effects of heating and air conditioning.

Panel Magic gives the shine of fine wood to your⁵ walls and preserves them for years to come. It leaves no oily, unattractive film and does not stain. It leaves only a⁶ pleasant fragrance for a few days.

For a free sample, mail the enclosed coupon. Yours very truly,   [137]

46 Dear Mr. Hunter: It gives me great pleasure to write you that you are one of the ten representatives in our¹ company who have sold over a million dollars' worth of life insurance during the past year. Your efforts have² earned you and your family a free trip to Hawaii. Congratulations on your great achievement!

You can³ take this trip any time

between May 15 and July 15. For complete details, please write Mr. Charles R. Brown[4] in the personnel department.

The past year has been a good one for our organization, and we are confident[5] that with the assistance of men like you, the coming year will be even better. Cordially yours,[6] [120]

47 Dear Mr. Smith: Thank you for your order for a Wilson pipe. It has been shipped, and you should receive it soon.

Your pipe[1] is a quality product. It was made by a skilled craftsman with the finest materials.

To obtain the best[2] results from your pipe, never remove the stem while the pipe is warm. Let the pipe stand until it is cool and fairly dry.[3] The Wilson expands with heat and moisture. Pulling out the stem at the wrong time may cause the shank to split.

Take care of[4] your pipe, and it will give you many years of enjoyment. Very truly yours, [94]

48 Dear Mr. Emerson: If you find one day that you need more warehouse space, think twice before you decide to build or[1] buy. You may be able to save yourself thousands of dollars by leasing rather than building or buying. Leasing[2] provides you with the space you need while it keeps your company's capital and credit intact. Leasing also offers[3] special tax benefits that are not available to you if you own a building.

The Hopkins Real Estate[4] Company specializes in finding commer-

cial buildings for companies that are about to expand. Learn[5] more about our service by sending for our informative brochure. We will send you one upon receipt of the[6] enclosed card. Very truly yours, [125]

49 Dear Mr. Downs: My family and I were thrilled to learn that I had won a free trip to Hawaii in this year's[1] life insurance sales contest. We have always wanted to visit Hawaii, but we have never had the[2] opportunity.

There is, however, one problem. You stated that we must take this trip sometime within the next two months.[3] Unfortunately, I am scheduled to have surgery in three weeks. It is unlikely that I will have recovered[4] sufficiently to go to Hawaii within the two-month period.

Would it be possible for me to get[5] an extension in the time that we can take the trip? If not, might we receive the equivalent amount of the[6] cost of the trip in cash? Sincerely yours, [127]

LESSON 7

54 Dear Mrs. Smith: After checking our records, we find that you are correct in stating that there is a mistake in[1] the bill we sent you several days ago. We should have billed you for $50 instead of $60.[2] You will find a corrected statement enclosed.

We are very sorry about this error, Mrs. Smith, and will be[3] more careful in the future.

Won't you drop in our store the next time you are in downtown Miami to see our new[4] line of fall merchandise. The members of our large, well-trained staff are eager to serve you. Sincerely yours, [98]

55 Dear Mr. Drake: One of the great needs today in preparing young people to become competent stenographers[1] is to improve their proficiency in grammar usage. You will find that *Communications in Today's Business*[2] is the most effective book on the market to prepare your students to use good grammar in business communications.[3]

The author, Dr. Janet Green, has a fine background in business writing. She has been a professor of[4] business for a number of years and has done a great deal of research in this field.

With her excellent background, Dr.[5] Green has written a book that has been long needed for teaching writing skills.

If you would like to receive an[6] examination copy of *Communications in Today's Business*, return the enclosed card. After you have examined[7] it, we are confident you will want to use it in your classes. Sincerely yours, [156]

56 Gentlemen: On January 7 I ordered a set of flatware by telephone from your Boston store. The[1] shipment was to have been delivered to me within one week. Today is February 1, and I have not yet[2] received the flatware. Will you please check into this matter for me.

My name, account number at your store, and the flatware[3] stock number from the catalog are shown at the bottom of this letter.

Please let me know if you can trace this[4] order. Otherwise, I will consider it canceled. Yours very truly, [93]

57 Dear Mr. Taylor: Thank you for accepting our invitation to speak at the meeting sponsored by the Iowa[1] Businessmen's Club. The suggested title of your talk, "How to Build Goodwill," is certainly appropriate for[2] this occasion.

As I mentioned in my previous letter, the meeting will be held on Saturday, May 10. Dinner[3] will be served at 7 p.m., and your speech will follow. The dinner will be held in Room 102 at Des Moines[4] High School.

If there is any way in which we can be of help to you as you prepare your speech, please let us know.[5]

We are eager to hear your speech. Sincerely yours, [109]

58 Dear Mr. Norton: This year a small college won't cut the lawns as often as it has in the past. Next year it may[1] cut out one of its athletic teams. When money is scarce, a school begins to eliminate things. If cash does not[2] come in, then more and more things must be eliminated.

Colleges throughout the country are in financial trouble.[3] In the last two years, 22 colleges have closed. The reason is that tuition pays for only a third of[4] the cost of a college education. The rest has to come from sources such as contributions from people like[5] you.

Even with 22 colleges gone, there are still over 1,500 that need your help. Won't you please give[6] now to the college of your choice. Sincerely yours, [129]

59 Dear Mrs. Cambridge: We are particularly happy to acknowledge your letter of Friday, March 20,[1] telling us that you will pay your bill no later than June 1 with three separate payments of $100[2] each.

If you are able to make these payments at monthly intervals as you suggest, this will be satisfactory[3] to us. We will expect to receive your final payment on or before June 1.

We know you realize, Mrs.[4] Cambridge, that your credit rating depends upon the way you pay your bills. If for any reason you cannot[5] make the payments as stated, please let us know promptly. Very truly yours, [113]

LESSON 8

63 Dear Mr. Jackson: As you requested, we are returning to you the questionnaire you sent us a few days ago[1] regarding current major television programs. We have made an effort to give you an honest answer[2] to each question.

May I suggest that the stations offer more variety in daytime programming on the weekends.[3] Many of the daytime programs are cartoons and sports that do not, in our opinion, meet the viewing needs of[4] the complete audience.

Thank you very much for the opportunity to express our opinion. Sincerely[5] yours, [101]

64 Dear Mr. Smith: Will your next direct-mail piece make the proper impression on those who receive it? What paper you[1] put it on and what envelope you put it in can definitely make a difference.

At the National Paper[2] Company we never forget this difference. We believe that this is the main reason why we are the largest[3] suppliers of papers and envelopes to the direct-mail industry.

National papers are suitable[4] for folders, brochures, reports, letters, and any other promotion piece that has to make a good impression.

Won't[5] you give us the opportunity sometime soon, Mr. Smith, to show you our complete line of National products.[6] Sincerely yours, [122]

65 Dear Mr. Gates: When you need a truck expert, we have "four on the floor." Four truck specialists at James and Company[1] spend every working day helping people like you get the right truck for their needs.

Do you want to know whether you[2] should buy, lease, or rent? Are you wondering where to get technical advice? Or do you have other questions concerning[3] heavy truck service?

Any one of our four truck specialists can solve these problems for you. James and Company[4] can provide you with the following:

1. A big inventory of new and used trucks available for immediate[5] delivery.

2. Flexible lease and rental plans for all trucks.

3. A complete, well-equipped service department[6] staffed by factory-trained technicians.

Our "four on the floor" tackle problems, and they solve them, too. Give us an[7] opportunity to prove this to you, Mr. Gates. Yours very truly,   [153]

66 Dear Professor Tyler: Thank you for your inquiry about employment opportunities at the Hunter Import[1] and Export Company. Yes, we do have an opening in the personnel department at this time. The young[2] man you described in your letter seems to be very well qualified for the job. We are especially interested[3] in the employment tests in shorthand, typewriting, and grammar that he prepared while he was in college.

If[4] he is interested in the position, please ask him to get in touch with Mr. Peters, supervisor of our[5] personnel department, to arrange for an interview.

Thank you for telling us about this young man. Cordially[6] yours, [121]

67 Dear Friend: You can get all the comfort you want without buying a larger car than you need. There was a time when the[1] only way you could get a really fine car was to buy a big one.

That is no longer true. When you want a[2] fine car today, there is a new medium-sized Star that will fit your needs perfectly.

The Star illustrates beautifully[3] that comfort does not have to be measured by size.

The interior proves that full-sized cars do not have a[4] monopoly on comfort. The best example of the Star's elegance is the seating. Foam padding and rich fabrics[5] cover the spacious bucket or bench seats.

We want you to enjoy all this comfort. Drop by your nearest Star dealer[6] today; you will be glad you did. Sincerely yours, [130]

68 Dear Martha: On Friday, June 15, John and I are planning to have a small dinner party as a farewell to[1] my daughter Jane. As you may have heard, Jane accepted a position with the United Nations and will be stationed[2] in Brussels. She leaves on June 18. As you can imagine, she is quite excited.

If you and Fred can join[3] us at this party, we will be delighted to have you. Dinner will be at seven. Sincerely yours, [78]

69 Dear Mr. Fisher: It was a pleasure to have you at the Governor Smith Hotel several days ago. We[1] hope that you were pleased with our facilities and with our services.

We earnestly desire to maintain a[2] courteous, friendly atmosphere in our hotels. Won't you help us in our efforts to do so by filling out and returning[3] the enclosed questionnaire telling us what you particularly liked about our services. If there was anything[4] you did not like, we would also like to know that. It will take you only a few minutes to fill out the[5] questionnaire.

We will appreciate your cooperation. Very truly yours, [114]

LESSON 9

73 Dear Mr. Bailey: It is my understanding that the Dane County Fair is scheduled for the last week of

August.[1] The Central College Business Club would like to prepare an exhibit for this fair.

The main purpose of our club[2] is to encourage students to prepare for careers in business, and we would appreciate the opportunity[3] to show the people of Dane County some of our projects.

If you can assign a space for our club, please let us[4] know as soon as possible so that we will have time to prepare an interesting exhibit.

Thank you for your[5] consideration. Sincerely yours, [103]

74 Dear Mr. Wilson: I am happy to be able to give you a favorable report on Miss Mary James, the[1] young lady who has applied for a position with your organization.

Miss James worked with Mr. Green and me[2] from 1968 until last year. She did a fine job for us but left us to finish her college degree.[3]

We found her to be a hardworking, conscientious person who was never afraid to assume new responsibilities.[4] I wish we could take her back, but we do not have an opening at the present time.

I am sure that[5] Miss James will be able to handle capably any position that you entrust to her. Very truly yours,[6] [120]

75 Dear Mr. Jones: Thank you for your letter accepting our offer to represent our company in Massachusetts,[1] New Hampshire, and Vermont. This territory has not been covered for some time, and it offers fine opportunities[2] for new business.

I am sending you separately a copy of our sales manual. It outlines our sales[3] policies and describes our principal markets. After you have read it, I will be glad to answer any questions[4] you may have.

I am confident, Mr. Jones, that your coverage of this territory will work to our mutual[5] advantage. Yours very truly, [104]

76 Dear Mr. Potts: For many years I have observed the fine work that the Brownfield Home for the Aged is doing in[1] our community. As a matter of fact, a very close friend of mine, Mrs. Alice Burlington, is presently[2] a resident of your home, and I have occasion to visit her from time to time. From these contacts, I have[3] had an opportunity to observe closely the fine work you are doing.

Since I believe you are providing[4] a wonderful service to the community, I am enclosing my check for $500 as a[5] contribution to the operation of the home. The money may be used for whatever purpose you desire, but[6] I hope it will be spent to provide the residents with a little extra in the way of recreational[7] facilities.

Congratulations on the excellent job you are doing. Sincerely yours, [157]

77 Dear Mr. Lester: The Eastern Chemical Association offers its members three valuable services:[1]

1. A year's subscription to our quarterly magazine, *The American Chemist*.

2. A copy of our yearbook,[2] published every spring, in which latest

developments in the chemical world are discussed.

3. Privileges[3] to attend all the meetings of the annual convention in Buffalo, New York.

It is the hope of your[4] officers that all members may enjoy these privileges, but to do so they must send in their dues soon. This year the dues[5] are only $3. Why not send us your check now. While you are about it, make a note of the convention dates.[6] They are April 11, 12, and 13. Yours very truly,   [133]

78 Dear Miss Ray: Because we believe that your hair deserves the best possible care, we are offering you an opportunity[1] to attend a special class on the subject of hair care. In this class you will have an opportunity[2] to learn the right way to take care of your particular type of hair. You will also have an opportunity[3] to consult with the instructor about any special hair problems you may have.

The class will be held on[4] January 5 from 3 to 5 p.m. at the Baker Hotel. The cost is only $5.

As we can[5] accommodate only 50 persons, make your reservation without delay if you are interested. Simply[6] call us at 141-2589.

Don't miss this opportunity to learn how to give your hair the care it[7] deserves. Cordially yours,   [143]

79 Dear Ellen: Fred and I will be delighted to take part in the farewell party for your daughter Jane. We will arrive[1] at seven.

I had not heard that Jane took a job with the United Nations. I am very

happy for her.[2] With her training in foreign affairs, that type of job was made for her. Cordially yours,   [55]

80 Dear Mr. West: As you know, the annual Business Machines Show will be held in Milwaukee on December 18,[1] 19, and 20 at the Hotel Brown. At this show we will display our new line of copying machines,[2] electronic calculators, and electric typewriters.

Please accept the enclosed two tickets to the show with our[3] compliments. If you would like to have additional tickets, do not hesitate to let us know.

We look forward[4] to seeing you at the show. Sincerely yours,   [88]

LESSON 10

83 *GNP—Scorecard of Progress*

How exactly does one measure the soundness of a national economy? What kind of yardstick do economists[1] and politicians use? As yardsticks go, few have greater status than one called Gross National Product—known[2] familiarly as GNP.

A concise definition of the term goes like this: GNP is the total[3] market value of all the goods and services produced in a country in a given year. Stated another[4] way, it is the value in dollars of all goods (cars, hairpins, clothes, and so on) and services (telephone calls,[5] salaries, and so on) sold in one year. According to the Department of Commerce, the GNP "serves as our[6] country's annual production-wise scorecard."

A word of caution is appropriate,

however. The figure we use[7] for the GNP is based on current prices. Since prices change from year to year, it may not be accurate to[8] compare the 1950 GNP with the present year's GNP without making adjustments. Ten dollars in 1950 could buy much more than ten dollars today. Therefore, today's[9] GNP would be higher than in 1950 even if the economy had remained at a standstill.[10]

For short spans of two or three years, however, the GNP's can be compared directly if there have been no[11] great changes in prices. Such comparisons can give a reasonably accurate picture of the growth (or[12] decline) of the economy.

By subtracting one year's GNP from the previous year's, we arrive at the amount of[13] growth (or decline) for the whole economy. From these figures, we can judge more accurately how the economy[14] has reacted to various conditions or specific policies. From these lessons, both the[15] government and businessmen can formulate policies for the future. For example, on the basis of the growth[16] rate, the federal government may decide how large the national budget could or should be. At the same time, individual[17] businessmen may decide whether to expand output or hold the line.

All this is fine on a national[18] scale, the average person might say, but what does the GNP have to do with the individual? When the[19] GNP tells him that the nation's economy is growing, he stands a good chance of sharing in the benefits[20] of increasing production. Individual citizens may see those benefits in the form of more jobs[21] and more products.

One important component of the GNP is Personal Income (PI)—arrived at by[22] subtracting from the Gross National Product taxes, retained profits, and other sums of money which do not belong[23] to the normal "spending-and-earning cycle." The PI represents the total of all income earned by all[24] the John and Jane Does in the United States. If we divide this total by the number of people in the[25] United States, we come up with the per capita income.

Of course, this figure bears little relation to any[26] particular individual's income. He or she may be earning much more or less than the national figure[27] cited. But it does give us an index of how well we are doing—whether we are getting richer, poorer,[28] or standing still. It is also a useful yardstick for comparing the living standards of different nations.[29]

Such yardsticks as the GNP, PI, and per capita income are based on concrete facts. They are drawn from the[30] many financial transactions which take place in our free enterprise economy. Because of this— because they[31] are not just vague estimates—they are especially reliable tools for the economist. [637] —Adapted from "GNP—Scorecard of Progress," *Senior Scholastic*, (Oct. 21, 1964).

84 Dear Mr. West: We sincerely feel that leasing a truck makes a lot more sense than owning one. However, we don't[1] expect you to take our word for it. That is why we are offering our new 90-day trial lease.

This lease gives[2] you all the advantages of long-term leasing. There is one big difference, however. If at the end of 90[3] days you find that leasing is not compatible with your particular needs, you can cancel your lease.

Isn't[4] this a fair offer? Why not take advantage of it. You have everything to gain and nothing to lose. Yours truly,[5]   [100]

85 Dear Mrs. Green: It is just about time to start Christmas shopping. That means, of course, that you will have lots of things[1] to remember and lots of extra things to do. Perhaps you, like most of us,

find that writing down the things you have[2] to do helps. If so, you will find the enclosed little memorandum pad useful. It is just the right size for a[3] pocket or a purse.

We hope it will remind you, too, that the National Service Station is right in your neighborhood[4] and is ready to help whenever your car needs service.

National keeps your car out of trouble. We spot minor[5] problems before they become major repairs. Our thorough service and fine products are designed to keep your car[6] running smoothly. Sincerely yours,
               [124]

Chapter 3

LESSON 11

89 Dear Mr. Logan: We were interested to learn that your company is considering the purchase of a[1] jet plane for the use of your executives. We are glad to tell you of our experience with the three planes we[2] purchased several years ago.

We have found that our executives are now able to make better use of their[3] time. They can travel from one of our branches to another without losing valuable time making reservations,[4] waiting for their luggage, and getting to and from large airports.

In addition, the purchase of these planes has enabled[5] us to increase the sale of our merchandise substantially.

If there are any other questions I can answer[6] for you about our experiences with our own planes, please write or call me. Yours very truly,   [138]

90 Dear Mr. Johnson: The information concerning the use your company has made of three Wilson jets is most[1] welcome. We have now reached a firm decision to purchase a plane for the use of our executives, and the Wilson[2] is one of those we are considering.

Although we have a great deal of information from the manufacturers[3] of the Wilson, we would appreciate more specific information from a present user of the[4] plane. Naturally, we are particularly interested in the cost of operation. If you will give[5] us information about the cost in each of the categories listed below, it would be most helpful.

1.[6] The number and cost of the personnel necessary to operate each plane.

2. Fuel and other operating[7] costs.

3. Hangar and other storage costs. Sincerely yours, [152]

91 Dear Mr. Logan: Our comptroller, who made an extensive study of the advantages of company-owned[1] planes, prepared the enclosed report for our board of directors. The report gives accurate, detailed information[2] on the cost of operating and maintaining these planes over a period of three years.

I am sure, Mr.[3] Logan, that you will find in this report the answers to the questions you raised in your letter of April 15.[4]

If we can provide any additional information, please call us. Sincerely yours, [96]

92 Dear Mr. Billings: Thank you for renewing your air express contract with us. We are glad that you will continue[1] using our service.

In the next few months we will receive two new Star jets. These planes, which were designed especially[2] for us, will accommodate much larger and heavier shipments. When these planes are in operation, we will be[3] able to give you even better service than we have in the past. Sincerely yours, [75]

93 Dear Mr. Day: I have gone over the brief you prepared requesting airline service to your city, and it appears[1] to be quite comprehensive. Our board, which will meet on November 16, will consider the points you raise in[2] the brief. No doubt your commissioner, Mr. Harry Rose, has informed you of our recommendation that each[3] community desiring airline service arrange its own exhibit of materials.

We are planning a meeting[4] of witnesses starting at 9:30 a.m. on Monday, January 21. Please make a special[5] effort to have one of your representatives attend. Very truly yours, [114]

94 Dear Mr. Jones: Mr. Green was suddenly called out of town because of the illness of our plant manager in[1] Mobile. The date of his return is indefinite, but he will probably be gone about three weeks.

Before he[2] left, he asked me to write you that he has not yet had an opportunity to read the contracts you sent him[3] but that he will study them as soon as he returns. I hope that everything is going well with you. Sincerely yours,[4] [80]

95 Dear Mr. Knight: On Friday, June 16, we filed an application with the proper government agency to[1] discontinue service temporarily at Rockville because of the small amount of business there. Yesterday[2] we received a letter from the agency giving us the necessary permission.

Consequently, we plan[3] to terminate service at Rockville on August

21. The last flight will be No. 211 to Chicago[4] leaving at 6 p.m.

We are sorry *to* discontinue this service, but we have no alternative. Sincerely[5] yours, [101]

LESSON 12

100 Dear Mr. Riley: Because of a substantial decrease in our volume of business in Portland since 1970,[1] we find it necessary to discontinue service to that city and to close our office at[2] 6134 Third Avenue. Therefore, we must terminate our agreement No. 1156 under which you[3] provide transportation to and from the airport serving Portland. Our check for $1,450[4] is enclosed to take care of the balance of our account.

We hope to be able to resume service to Portland[5] sometime in the future. We would then, of course, wish to enter into a new agreement with you.

Throughout the[6] years that the present agreement has been in effect, you have provided us with prompt, efficient service. Thank you[7] for the fine job you have done, Mr. Riley. Very truly yours, [152]

101 Dear Mr. Long: Your announcement that you are discontinuing airfreight service to Fort Worth was both a surprise[1] and a disappointment. We had not realized that the volume of business had decreased to such an extent that[2] you would contemplate discontinuing service.

You did not mention in your letter the exact date that you are[3] terminating service. We hope, however, that it will not be before March 30.

This will give us time to find[4] other shipping facilities.

We have enjoyed using your services for the past three years, and we sincerely[5] hope that you will resume them in the near future. Sincerely yours, [113]

102 Dear Mr. Kelly: Thank you very much for your letter requesting information about the New Orleans School[1] of Aviation. We are sending you separately our catalog No. 1986, which lists all the courses[2] we offer and the cost of each.

Most of our students obtain their flying licenses within a year, but we[3] have had several who have completed the required course work and flying time much sooner.

After you have had an[4] opportunity to look over the catalog, I will be happy to answer any questions you may have.[5] Just call me at 788-8999. Sincerely yours, [111]

103 Dear Mr. Ray: Your recent letter concerning the legal aspects of purchasing a used airplane has been referred[1] to me. There are a number of things that you should keep in mind.

When you are completing arrangements to buy your plane,[2] be sure to examine closely the current registration or have a title company investigate the[3] matter for you. Whenever a plane changes hands, federal regulations require that a record of the sale[4] be filed with the Aviation Commission. The regulation handbook states, "If the bill of sale you receive is[5] not from the last owner of record, the commission considers the sale invalid and will not recognize it."6

Clearing up such a defective title is costly, time-consuming, and frustrating. It is much simpler, therefore,7 to check on the registration before you sign a contract of sale.

If I can be of further help to you, please8 let me know. Sincerely yours, [165]

104 Dear Mr. Budd: Mr. Taylor is away on a short vacation, but I will call your letter to his attention1 as soon as he returns on August 10.

I have checked his calendar and find that he must attend a meeting2 of the board of directors of the National Aviation Company on August 15, the day you would3 like to have luncheon with him. However, he is free on August 16. Would that day be convenient for you? I4 am tentatively reserving that day on his calendar. Cordially yours, [94]

105 Dear Mr. Riley: On July 20 I flew on Central Airlines Flight 112 from Salt Lake City to St.1 Louis. The service I received on this flight was exceptional, and I feel I should express my gratitude.

My2 connecting flight from Reno to Salt Lake City was delayed *by* mechanical problems. When I arrived in Salt3 Lake City, I rushed to the gate to board Flight 112, but the airplane door had already been closed.

I asked the4 agent at the gate if *it* would be possible to let me board the plane even though I was late. The agent called5 the pilot, who agreed to open the door and let me

aboard. This thoughtful action on his part saved me several6 hours' time and a great deal of inconvenience.

Thank you for your fine service. Cordially yours, [136]

LESSON 13

109 Dear Captain Russell: As a result of the interest created by last year's trip, the travel committee of1 our organization is again planning a trip to Spain. All members and their families are urged to take2 advantage of this trip.

The cost, which includes air fare, hotel accommodations, and transportation to and from all3 airports, is only $500 per person.

The trip is scheduled for the last two weeks of July. You can4 obtain further information if you will write to Mr. John Barton, chairman of the travel committee.

If5 you wish to reserve space on this trip, send us your deposit at the rate of $50 per person by June6 1. Final payment is due on July 1. Sincerely yours, [131]

110 Dear Mr. Barton: My family and I would like to take the chartered trip to Spain, which I understand is planned1 for the last two weeks in July. Please reserve four places for me and my family. My personal check No.2 1156 for $200 is enclosed.

I would appreciate it if you would send me a complete3 listing of the cities and points of interest that we will visit. Sincerely yours, [75]

111 Gentlemen: We have recently learned that your airline may be

denied permission to operate at the Midvale[1] airport. Naturally, this is a very disturbing development to the citizens and businessmen of[2] Midvale.

It is our opinion that the service your airline renders to Midvale contributes immeasurably[3] to the development and progress of the city. Consequently, we have formed a committee to do everything[4] possible to help keep your air service in Midvale.

According to a report in yesterday's newspaper,[5] hearings on this matter are scheduled for Thursday, November 12. Fifteen or twenty members of our committee[6] intend to be present at this meeting. Please let us know how we can cooperate with you to the fullest extent.[7] Cordially yours,   [142]

112 Dear Mr. Smith: Your letter indicating the concern of the citizens of Midvale about the possibility[1] that our airline will be denied the privilege of operating in your city was most welcome. We[2] appreciate very much the support of the members of your committee, and we extend to them a cordial invitation[3] to attend the hearings on Thursday, November 12.

Enclosed is a memorandum that contains detailed[4] information on the location and time of the hearings.

We look forward to seeing you on November[5] 12. Sincerely yours,
[103]

113 Dear Mr. Newton: I understand that you are planning to install new facilities to provide gasoline[1]

for jet planes at the Birmingham airport. Would you please tell me the proposed location of the new refueling[2] facilities.

As you may know, the present location is inconvenient for our four-engine jets. When the new facilities[3] are installed, we naturally hope that a larger, more convenient location will be selected.[4] We realize, of course, that any installation will have to satisfy the requirements of the airport[5] authorities. You have undoubtedly given a great deal of thought to this matter and have discussed it with the airport[6] manager.

We will appreciate your forwarding to us a diagram of the proposed location of[7] the new refueling facilities if one is available. Yours very truly,   [155]

114 Dear Mr. Smith: When you fly on International Airlines, you no longer have to have your meals at your seat. You[1] can have them in the dining room on our international flights. We are the only airline that offers you this[2] convenience.

When dinner is over, the dining room converts into a first-class lounge where you can relax, play cards,[3] and listen to music.

Of course, if you still prefer to eat at your seat, you can do so. But if all the compliments[4] that we have been getting from our first-class passengers are any indication, we are sure you will wind up[5] in our dining room.

The next time you plan to fly abroad, call our reservations desk and tell our clerk that you would[6] like to make a reservation for dinner in our dining room. Our telephone number is 116-1189.[7] Cordially yours, [144]

115 Dear Mr. Miller: Thank you for your inquiry concerning the location of refueling facilities[1] at the Birmingham airport. Enclosed is a diagram of the proposed location of these new facilities.[2] Twelve new pumps are planned, and they should greatly increase efficiency at the terminal. Let me say, however, that[3] the plans are tentative at this stage.

We suggest that we meet on Friday, July 16, at 9 a.m. to make[4] final plans if it is convenient for you.

If you have any objections to this proposal, please call me before[5] the meeting next Friday. Sincerely yours, [106]

LESSON 14

119 Dear Mr. Ford: Our Flight 103 is the most convenient daytime jet to London. Flight 103 leaves New York[1] daily at 10 a.m.; consequently, you can enjoy a full night's sleep at home the night before. Only six hours[2] after boarding Flight 103, you are in London. You land in time for an evening stroll along the banks of[3] the Thames.

Plan to get the most out of your trip to London; insist on a seat on Flight 103.

Our courteous,[4] efficient agents will be glad to make reservations for you. Sincerely yours, [94]

120 Dear Mr. Day: We are sorry that it was necessary for us to cancel Flight 161 from New York to[1] Chicago on June 15, but the fog was so heavy in New York on that day that we were unable to take[2] off.

New weather forecasting techniques and developments in instrument landing have helped us reduce cancellations[3] and delays to a great extent; however, there are still times when they cannot be avoided if we are to[4] protect the safety of our passengers.

We hope, Mr. Day, that you will give us another opportunity[5] to serve you when you fly on the routes we serve. We are confident you will have a pleasant, delightful trip. Sincerely[6] yours, [121]

121 Dear Mr. Drew: We understand that your organization, the National Association of Advertisers,[1] will hold its annual meeting this year in Chicago on December 26, 27, and 28.[2] We would like to offer you our services in making this year's meeting the best attended ever.

We[3] are confident that many more members would attend your meeting if they knew how easily and conveniently[4] they can get to Chicago by Swift Airlines. Swift operates in numerous cities in the United States from[5] which there is direct service to Chicago. By flying to Chicago, your members will have more time for recreation.[6]

If you will provide us with a current roster of your membership, we will send each person a convenient[7] flight schedule. Sincerely yours, [144]

122 Gentlemen: On Tuesday, June 16, I traveled on your airline from

New York to Pittsburgh. When my bag was delivered[1] to me in Pittsburgh, I found that it had been badly damaged; there were three or four scratches in the leather. As[2] the bag was in perfect condition when I checked it in New York, the damage must have occurred while it was in your[3] custody.

Will you please let me know what procedure I should follow to be compensated for the damage to[4] the bag. It seems to me that the only fair adjustment would be the replacement of my bag, which I had purchased[5] less than two months ago. I see no way to have the scratches repaired satisfactorily.

May I hear from you[6] soon. Yours very truly, [124]

123 Dear Mr. Smith: Some businessmen think that German Airlines serves only Germany. Actually, German Airlines[1] flies to over 100 cities in 64 countries. Altogether, we fly more than 86,000[2] miles of cargo routes, more than any other airline in the world.

We fly cargo to all parts of the world, and we[3] do it with efficiency and reliability that can save you a lot of worry, time, and money.

The[4] next time you have something to ship somewhere in this wide world, call German Airlines. Sincerely yours, [97]

124 Dear Mr. Brown: The demand for seats on our New York to Los Angeles flights has increased to such an extent in[1] the last three months that we have decided to add four more jet flights to our schedule beginning June 1.

Our entire[2] service between New York and Los Angeles is given in the enclosed timetable.

When you have to fly coast to[3] coast, let us arrange your transportation for you. Our travel department personnel will be delighted to serve[4] you. Yours very truly, [84]

125 Dear Mr. Day: We were sorry to learn that your bag was badly scratched when you picked it up at the Pittsburgh airport.[1] Our personnel are trained *to* handle luggage carefully, but occasionally a piece of luggage will be damaged[2] in spite of our best efforts.

Before we can make an adjustment, we will need the information called for on[3] the enclosed form. Please fill out this form and return it to us. As soon as we receive the form, we will take care of your[4] claim.

We are confident that the next time *you* fly via Western Airlines, Mr. Day, your luggage will arrive in[5] first-class condition. Sincerely yours, [107]

LESSON 15

128 *A Trip to France*

Each year, millions of Americans spend long periods of time considering the advantages and disadvantages[1] of the various trips presented in travel folders they have accumulated. Family budgets[2] are often limited, but this does not detract from the enjoyment people derive from reading about far-off[3] places so attractively illustrated and described in the literature produced by the transportation[4] media. The annual search for something out of the ordinary to do during the vacation period[5] adds to the zest of the vacation itself.

The low-cost airline services now available make it[6] possible to consider trips that previously were impossible because of time limitations. High among[7] the possibilities is a flight to France.

You can relax in the scenic splendor of the Old World and revel[8] in the art masterpieces; you can enjoy colorful native pageants, quaint customs, and beautiful costumes.[9]

When you fly across the Atlantic, you save precious days of that all-too-short vacation. You will have more time in[10] which to become familiar with the character and ideas of a different culture.

The fame and allure[11] of Paris captures your imagination and becomes the focal point of your trip. A call to your local travel[12] agent finds him ready to help you plan your trip. Your flight is in a fast, comfortable jetliner that soars[13] high above the weather. The latest navigational aids assist experienced pilots in carrying you[14] safely and smoothly to your destination at close to the speed of sound. Delicious complimentary meals are[15] served while you are aloft.

With the congenial atmosphere that prevails on these flights, you are soon carrying on an[16] interesting conversation about a variety of subjects with other passengers. Before you know[17] it, the "Fasten seat belts" sign flashes on. In minutes you are touching down on the runway and taxiing to the[18] terminal. The pressurized cabin of your plane and the skill of the pilot have brought you through a descent of many[19] thousand feet with no physical discomfort. Your travel agent's courteous representative meets you at[20] your destination with the friendly greeting, "May I help you?" He helps you through customs and with the necessary,[21] but perplexing, exchange of American dollars for French francs.

Perhaps you read about the layout of the city[22] of Paris as you were planning your trip. If you have not, you will be interested to know that the Seine flows[23] about eight miles within the city.

On the north side of the city you will find the business districts and the[24] residential section of the wealthy class. On the south side of the river is the Latin Quarter, so named because[25] years ago, when Latin was considered the language of the educated people, students at the nearby University[26] of Paris would go through the streets singing Latin songs.

Of course, like most tourists, you will want to visit[27] the historic places. You should include a visit to the Eiffel Tower, the Cathedral of Notre Dame, and[28] the Louvre Museum to see the "Mona Lisa."

A trip to France by plane can be one of the most rewarding[29] experiences of a lifetime.   [584]

129 Dear Mr. Keith: Fads spread around the country these days faster

than measles in grade school—and these fads are not confined[1] to any one age group.

If you rely on surface transportation to deliver your merchandise, you may find[2] that your competitor has already met the demand for the latest fad just about the time you get it in[3] stock.

Coastal Airfreight can help you take advantage of fads. We will send a truck to your plant to pick up your merchandise.[4] The truck will deliver it to the airport, where it will be placed aboard one of our freighters. Your merchandise[5] will reach its destination the next day, in time to capitalize on the fad.

We have more jet freighters connecting[6] major cities than any other airline.

Let us tell you how shipping merchandise by airfreight can increase[7] your profits. Return the enclosed card. Cordially yours, [150]

130 Dear Mr. Jones: Did you ever wish you owned your own airplane? Then instead of waiting for the plane, the plane waits for[1] you. If your meeting in, say, Dallas ends 20 minutes early, you can leave in your plane 20 minutes earlier.[2] If your meeting runs an hour late, you can take off an hour later. You fly where and when you want to, with no[3] stopovers or connecting flights.

Thousands of businessmen and women own their own planes. How about you? If you would[4] like to fly when and where you want to, get the complete story about Wilson jet planes. Just mail the enclosed card. When[5] we receive it, we will mail you a brochure that will show you that owning your own plane costs less than you might think. Sincerely[6] yours, [122]

Chapter 4

LESSON 16

134 Dear Mr. Lamb: We understand you when you say that you are a busy man. That is good because, after all, being[1] busy got you where you are today. You know the benefits of dedication and work.

Yet the successful[2] man is often too busy to give his investments all the time and attention they deserve. That is what National[3] investment management is all about. For a very small fee, one of our investment specialists will work[4] with you to manage your entire investment portfolio. We will supervise your investments, safeguard your assets,[5] and keep accurate accounting records, all within the framework of your financial objectives. And it will[6] take almost none of your valuable time.

May we suggest, Mr. Lamb, that you look into our program soon. We[7] have quite a success story to tell. Call Mrs. Judy Johnson, manager of our trust and investment division,[8] today. She will show you how to save time and make money. Sincerely yours, [174]

135 Dear Mr. Smith: Whether you

are a big investor or a small one, the National Investment Company offers[1] you a wide range of personal and business investment opportunities.

We will arrange for you an investment[2] plan that takes into consideration your cash needs for emergencies, insurance protection for you and[3] your family, and securities to hedge against inflation.

Our representative will be glad to tell you[4] about our plan. Why not invite him to do so. Simply indicate on the enclosed card the time he may call. Very[5] truly yours,   [102]

136 Dear Mr. Hastings: We will soon be moving! As you may have heard, the First National Bank is planning a new building[1] on which construction is scheduled to begin soon.

But before we can start to build our new banking office and[2] shopping complex, we will have to vacate our old building. Therefore, we will be temporarily located at[3] 1115 Main Street beginning May 15.

We will offer the same services you are accustomed to receiving[4] at our old location. In addition, we will have new drive-in facilities at the temporary[5] location.

We hope you will not find these new arrangements too inconvenient. We are excited about our new[6] building, and we will keep you posted as it takes shape.

In the meantime, won't you come in to see us in our temporary[7] location. Sincerely yours,   [147]

137 Dear Mr. Davis: When you are considering investments, don't overlook United States Savings Bonds. These bonds[1] are important to the stability of our nation's economy. Moreover, they are the safest investment[2] in the world.

At the First National Bank you can purchase two types of savings bonds—Series E and Series H.[3] Both earn the same rate of interest. With the Series E bonds, which increase in value every six months, you receive[4] all your interest when you cash the bonds. On the other hand, the Series H bonds yield interest semiannually,[5] which is paid to you in Treasury Department checks.

We urge you to consider adding to your personal[6] security by buying United States Savings Bonds. Sincerely yours,   [134]

138 Dear Mr. Jackson: Spring is on its way, and that is the time that many people start to think about buying new[1] cars. You can get a new car, Mr. Jackson, even though your funds may temporarily be low. How? Come into[2] any one of the branches of the County Trust Company and tell a member of our loan department that you[3] need money to buy a car. He will ask you a few questions and then recommend the plan that best meets your needs.

You[4] don't have to be a customer of the County Trust Company to get a car loan. But if you do have a checking[5] account with us, we can transfer your monthly car-loan payments from your checking account automatically.[6]

Come to see us soon and learn how easy it is to arrange a loan. Cordially yours,   [135]

139 Gentlemen: On Friday, November 12, Kenneth R. Baker passed away. The Springfield National Bank has been appointed[1] executor of his estate.

One of the documents that have been turned over to us is life insurance[2] policy 415615. Please let us know as soon as possible *the* value of this policy[3] at the time of Mr. Baker's death. We need this information in order to prepare the tax forms for the government.[4]

In addition, will you please forward to us any papers that must be filled *out* so that Mrs. Baker[5] can collect the principal sum of this policy. Very truly yours, [113]

LESSON 17

144 Dear Mr. Stone: You will be pleased to know that the Charleston Trust Company now has a new service available[1] to all depositors. Beginning June 5, two highly qualified, full-time trust officers will be available[2] to help you with any legal problems you may have concerning your will.

We think this service is an excellent[3] addition to the growing list of services that we offer. If you have not reviewed your will during the past[4] year or two, why not call today to make an appointment with one of our trust officers. He will be glad to help[5] you bring your will up to date. Cordially yours, [108]

145 Dear Mrs. Brown: Thank you for opening a savings account at the Delaware Savings Bank; we appreciate[1] your business.

Are you aware, Mrs. Brown, that our bank offers many other services in addition to those[2] available in the savings department? We invite you to take advantage of them. Enclosed is a four-page[3] folder describing all the services of the Delaware Savings Bank.

More than half our new business is the direct[4] result of recommendations made to others by well-satisfied depositors. Our depositors have[5] no hesitation in recommending us to their friends. We want you to feel that way too, and we will do everything[6] possible to make banking a genuine pleasure for you.

We are delighted to add your name to our[7] list of friends. We hope that this is the beginning of a pleasant, lasting friendship. Cordially yours, [157]

146 Dear Dr. James: As you know, the purchasing power of money changes. For many years we have seen the value of[1] the dollar shrink because of inflation. By putting some of your savings in stocks, which do not have a fixed value,[2] you can protect yourself against inflation. But the hard-pressed doctor, lawyer, or businessman never seems to have[3] time for the financial study necessary to invest wisely. That is why we recommend that you take advantage[4] of the helpful investment service offered by the Wilmington Trust Company.

The investment department[5] at the Wilmington Trust Company makes available to you the services of our well-trained staff of investment[6] specialists.

After you make arrangements for the Wilmington Trust Company to handle your investments,[7] you will have one less worry about the financial situation of your family in the future. Won't you[8] take a moment from your busy day to fill out and mail the enclosed reply card. When we receive it, one of our[9] investment counselors will arrange to meet with you at your convenience. Sincerely yours, [196]

147 Dear Mr. Harris: There is one important matter that you cannot afford to neglect—your will. If you have not[1] reviewed your will recently, you would be wise to do so without delay.

Because of its importance, your will should[2] be planned carefully. Furthermore, it should be reviewed regularly and revised in the light of today's economic[3] conditions, today's values, and recent changes in public laws. All these factors have a bearing upon[4] the final disposition you will want to make of your estate.

Why not stop in at the Virginia National[5] Bank soon and let our experienced officers help you review the provisions of your will.

You assume[6] no obligation by investigating the services we provide to help you with your estate problems. Cordially[7] yours, [142]

LESSON 18

151 Dear Mr. Long: We are happy to welcome you as a new checking account customer of ours.

Within the next[1] day or two you will receive a year's supply of checks and deposit slips free of charge. Your name and address are printed[2] on each of these checks and deposit slips. In addition, your account number is printed in magnetic ink[3] in the lower left corner.

Since your records are processed electronically, it is important that you use[4] only those checks and deposit slips that have your name and number printed on them.

We are pleased that you have chosen[5] the Lexington State Bank to serve you; we look forward to many years of friendship. Cordially yours, [117]

152 Dear Mr. Williams: Over the years the Commercial Credit Corporation has financed heavy construction equipment,[1] jet planes, machine tools, and even entire commercial fishing fleets.

We have also provided credit for[2] many small consumers that enabled them to enjoy the things they needed without having to wait for them. In[3] addition, we have helped distributors and retailers grow by financing their merchandise inventories.

As[4] you can see, we are specialists in a wide range of fields in which we provide tailor-made financing to fit people's[5] special needs. When you need financial help to buy a new car, a new house, or a new business, we can help[6] you. Yours very truly, [124]

153 Dear Mr. Green: It is a pleasure to answer your request for confidential information concerning Mr.[1]

James Brown's credit record.

Mr. Brown opened a checking account with us in 1968. Since that time[2] his balances at all times have met our minimum requirements for free banking services. In 1969[3] we granted Mr. Brown a loan of $1,000, and he made his payments promptly over a period[4] of a year.

For several years Mr. Brown was a correspondence supervisor for the Standard Products[5] Company in Wilmington. It is our understanding that several months ago he was appointed to the[6] position of head of the adjustment department of that company.

In our opinion, Mr. Brown may be[7] depended upon to meet his credit obligations; we have no hesitation giving him a good rating.[8] Very truly yours, [163]

154 Dear Mr. Becker: How do you manage money when you do not have much cash? Even though there is not much loose change[1] in your pocket, you may have quite a bit of money. This is particularly true if you have a house, some insurance,[2] a savings account, and perhaps other investments. This "money" may be on paper, but it is still yours and[3] needs careful attention. It needs good money management.

This is where our bank's services can help. We offer all[4] the usual banking services, of course. In addition, however, we have a full-time money management[5] department. This department stands ready at all times to advise you on any problems you may have concerning money.[6]

If you need help in managing your money, call us. Sincerely yours, [133]

155 Dear Mr. Day: Now that fall is just around the corner, the new cars will soon be available. No doubt the new[1] models this year will be among the most beautifully designed ever. If you are thinking of buying a new[2] car, why not let the North Carolina National Bank handle the financing for you. We offer the lowest[3] interest rates in town for financing automobiles.

To arrange a low-cost car loan, you need do only three things[4]:

1. Select the car that particularly appeals to you.

2. Discuss your needs with the head of our loan department.[5]

3. Choose the repayment plan that best fits your budget.

It's that easy. Sincerely, [114]

156 Dear Mr. Locke: Because of the severe winter we have just gone through, you may need to make some repairs on your home.[1] If your home has been damaged, you should protect your investment by taking care of this work immediately.

Perhaps[2] you contemplate doing some things to improve your home this spring—painting, roofing, or redecorating. *You* probably[3] wish to plan these jobs without delay before the summer's rush.

If you need a few hundred dollars or even[4] more to spend on repairs or remodeling, our loan department will be glad to make arrangements for a loan.[5] Our banking hours are from 9 a.m. to 4 p.m. from Monday through Friday. Sincerely yours, [117]

LESSON 19

160 Dear Mr. Harrington: A comparison of my financial records with the bank statement I received for the[1] month of April shows a discrepancy of $50. According to my records, my balance should be[2] $280 rather than $230.

Will you please examine my account to see if[3] you can find this error. If you would like me to return my canceled checks and statement, please let me know. Cordially[4] yours, [81]

161 Dear Mr. Sheaffer: Thank you for writing about the discrepancy of $50 between your records and[1] ours. We have made a complete check of our records of your account, but we have not found any error.

Please check your[2] records against our statement carefully again. If you do not find the error, please bring your records to our office;[3] we will be happy to go over them with you. Sincerely yours, [72]

162 Dear Mr. Niles: As you requested in your letter of August 29, we have closed your checking account No.[1] 11561 and have prepared a final statement. According to our records, your balance was[2] $1,115. A check for this sum is enclosed.

Thank you for the business your company has given us[3] in the past, Mr. Niles. Should you need banking facilities in Burlington in the future,

we hope you will reopen[4] your account with us. Very truly yours, [89]

163 To the Staff: Everybody wants to save money. Unfortunately, most people seem to have a difficult time[1] actually doing it. They start to save and then stop, and the money never seems to accumulate.

The[2] payroll savings plan is the easy, painless way to start saving and keep saving. Your money has a chance to[3] accumulate rapidly because the amount you specify is automatically set aside from your paycheck[4] and used to buy United States Savings Bonds.

Why not join our payroll savings plan. It is a practical, logical[5] way to make today's good intentions pay off tomorrow.

An application form is attached. Simply indicate[6] on it the amount you want deducted each month, initial it, and return it to the payroll department.[7] A. C. Jennings [143]

164 Dear Mr. Tarkington: As a result of the remodeling recently completed at our bank, we are now[1] able to offer our customers convenient drive-in banking service. Here are some of the things you can now do[2] without getting out of your car:

1. Make deposits and withdrawals
2. Cash checks
3. Make payments on loans

When you[3] have banking business to transact in the future, use one of our new drive-in windows. You will find this new service[4] fast and convenient. Very truly yours, [87]

165 Dear Mr. Parker: Thank you

for filling out our mortgage application form and for returning it so promptly.[1]

The people to whom you referred us all spoke very highly of you as a person of unquestioned character[2] and integrity.

Unfortunately, your present annual income of $10,000 causes us to[3] wonder whether a mortgage of $30,000 would not impose on you too big a financial burden.[4] Your monthly payments on this mortgage would come to $250. This amount, added to your ordinary[5] living expenses, would place a great strain on your budget.

If you have some other sources of income that[6] you did not report on our application form, please tell us about them. We will then be glad to reconsider[7] your request for a $30,000 mortgage. Sincerely yours, [153]

166 Dear Mr. Jones: It is a joy to know that a new baby is on the way, but a new baby can be a problem[1] if your home is too small.

If you are ever in that situation, let the Wilson National Bank solve your[2] problem with a home-improvement plan.

Under this plan, you can get up to $10,000 at low interest[3] rates, with terms that you can handle even after the baby arrives.

Of course, home-improvement loans aren't just to[4] help you get ready for a new baby. They can help you put in a new kitchen, an extra bedroom, or an outside[5] patio.

It is easy to apply for one of our home-improvement loans. Just stop in at our branch nearest[6] you. Yours very truly, [124]

167 Dear Mr. Drake: On Friday, June 15, we interviewed Mr. B. B. Miller for a position of responsibility[1] in the Chemical Bank of California. He has given us your name as a business[2] reference.

Mr. Miller stated that he was employed by the Wilmington National Bank for five years before he[3] moved to California. We would appreciate it, Mr. Drake, if you would give us your opinion *of* Mr.[4] Miller with regard to his ability to do high-level work on an independent basis. We would[5] also like to know whether you would hire him again if you were given the opportunity to do so.

We[6] will, of course, keep any information you give us confidential. Cordially yours, [134]

LESSON 20

170 *Money*

It has been praised as "sweeter than honey" and condemned as "the root of all evil." It is said to be a "good servant[1] but a poor master." Those who don't have it would usually like some. Those who have some would like more. Those who[2] have lots of it—well, they have their own problems.

The "it" in question is something we call money. In the long and often[3] fascinating history of money, everything from livestock to gold dust and seashells has been used as the[4] accepted medium of exchange at one time or another. In the United

States today there are only[5] two kinds of money circulated in significant amounts:

Currency. Paper or coins circulated by[6] the federal government.

Demand Deposits. Deposits in commercial banks against which checks can be drawn "on[7] demand." A person need not always pay his bills in currency; he can write a check against his deposit in[8] a bank. Indeed, this "checkbook money" is used to a far greater extent than currency. In fact, it accounts for[9] an estimated 80 percent of our country's money supply.

What gives value to money? Money is valuable[10] only because everyone agrees to accept it as a means of exchange. Consequently, it[11] can be readily exchanged for any kind of goods and services that people regard as "valuable." In[12] keeping with the economic laws of supply and demand, prices quickly rise when money is plentiful, and[13] the result is inflation. The reverse of all this, of course, is deflation. [274]—Adapted from "Money . . . Its Care and Nourishment," *Senior Scholastic*, (April 21, 1967).

171 *Where Does All the Money Go?*

Have you hidden any money lately? It seems as though everyone else has. One morning in Troy a few weeks[1] ago, a mill owner revealed on his deathbed that he had buried a fortune beneath his mill. Excavation[2] disclosed that he had stashed away $500,000 in old milk bottles.

Such secret caches are just one reason[3] why money vanishes. Currency and coins are constantly dis-appearing from circulation. Where do they[4] go? Examine a handful of pennies. You may not find one dated before 1935, and you will probably[5] find no Indian-head pennies. Yet before 1919, when Indian-head pennies were last minted,[6] they were issued by the billions. Where are they?

How long has it been since you received in change a Booker T. Washington[7] half-dollar? Did you ever receive one? Yet between 1946 and 1951, more than[8] 2,000,000 were made.

Some coin disappearances are temporary and local. When a bank messenger in Boston[9] recently went to the Federal Reserve Bank for ten bags of nickels, he returned with only one bag; nickels[10] were in short supply that day. Some money disappears permanently; it goes into private hoards. When an Iowa[11] woman ripped the back off an old mirror she had bought at an auction for a dollar, bills began cascading[12] out on the table. They were all large-sized bills, apparently from about the time of the Wall Street crash. The lady's[13] investment made her $1,000 richer.

From ancient times people have buried their money when they wanted[14] to hide it. Sometimes amazing burying sites have been chosen. A man stood at the bedside of his dying father[15] who, though paralyzed and unable to speak or write, was trying desperately to tell him something. He didn't[16] succeed. While the son was decorating his parents' graves the following Memorial Day, he dislodged from[17] his mother's grave several tins that contained something that looked like currency. The contents of the tins amounted[18] to $23,000.

Hiding large sums is unquestionably less common today than it used to be,[19] thanks to banks, credit cards, and charge accounts. Nevertheless, a good many people keep quite a bit of currency[20] hidden away. [402]

172 Dear Miss Gates: On April 15 the National Savings Bank will convert its accounting system to a computer[1] method.

This conversion will enable us to serve you faster and more efficiently. We will be able to[2] give you up-to-the-minute information about your account in a matter of minutes. The National Savings[3] Bank is the first one in the state to place its accounts on a computer. It is another illustration of[4] our efforts to give you the finest possible service.

The next time you are in the area of our bank, please[5] stop in and let us bring your passbook up to date. Sincerely yours, [112]

173 Dear Mr. Day: We have recently introduced a completely new service at the Wilson Bank—an international[1] officer. This officer's job is to handle your international banking and financial needs wherever[2] in the world they may be. This officer has at his disposal the vast knowledge and experience of[3] our foreign country specialists.

If you can use the services of this officer, call us at 118-6656.[4] His services are yours without charge. Cordially yours, [92]

Chapter 5

LESSON 21

177 Gentlemen: The General Computer Manufacturing Company is pleased to announce a seminar for[1] prospective users of our data processing equipment. It will be held at the Baker Institute in Chicago[2] on Friday morning, October 25, between the hours of nine and twelve.

The seminar will include[3] such subjects as accounting, merchandise control, and billing procedures. It will be of great value to businessmen[4] in both technical and managerial areas.

Please fill out and return the enclosed application[5] form if you wish to have any of your people attend. All applications must be in our hands by September[6] 15 at the latest. Cordially yours, [127]

178 Dear Mr. Fields: Enclosed is my application for the data processing seminar to be held at the Baker[1] Institute on the 25th of October.

As several other members of my department may also[2] wish to attend, I would appreciate receiving five additional application forms as well as a[3] copy of the complete program.

I would also like to know whether it will be possible to use a computer[4] in a "hands-on" simulation. Cordially yours, [90]

179 Dear Mr. Jones: Thank you for your inquiry of April 15 about our low-cost computer terminals. These[1] terminals, which can easily be installed in any business office, can handle most routine data processing[2] applications.

The computer terminal is connected by telephone lines to our main computer in[3] Stamford. You pay only for the time you actually use the computer.

The Stamford computer is a[4] General 4601 model with the capacity to handle numerous projects from various users[5] at the same time. It is a real-time, on-line computer that can cut your data processing costs substantially.[6]

If you would like to have further information or if you would like to visit our computer center in Stamford,[7] please let us know. Very cordially yours, [148]

180 Dear Mr. Atkins: Let us help you cut your office costs. The Systems Control Service can make an independent[1] study of your office operations and recommend many ways in which you can organize your work to make[2] substantial savings in time and cost.

We will be happy to make a free preliminary survey and give you[3] an estimate of our charge for a complete systems study.

If your business is large enough to support data[4] processing equipment, we can install just the right hardware to do an economical, efficient job for[5] you.

On January 20 I will be in Trenton and would like to visit your office during the afternoon.[6] I will phone you to find out whether that time is convenient for you. Very truly yours, [137]

181 Dear Mr. Lewis: On June 15, 1973, the marketing department of Central State College[1] began conducting a series of seminars on electronic data processing procedures in business.[2]

These seminars have been well received; we have had 30 requests to conduct such seminars in business offices.[3] Most of the requests have been from large retail businesses, but we have also heard from small banks, insurance companies,[4] and manufacturing plants.

Unfortunately, we cannot provide this off-campus service because of[5] a current staff shortage. We will, however, continue to offer these seminars at the college.

Enclosed is[6] a schedule of the seminars. If you would like to attend one of them, please let us know. Sincerely yours,[7] [140]

182 Dear Miss Preston: Your letter requesting information about a position in the field of data processing[1] education has been referred to me. At the present time we do not have an opening for a teacher[2] in this field.

The attached list gives the names and addresses of the colleges in this area that offer data[3] processing courses. It may be that one of them has an opening. Sincerely yours, [76]

183 Dear Mr. Day: We were happy to receive your inquiry about our data processing course. The class will meet[1] in Room 1515 of the Data Processing Center at Eastern State College. The first meeting will begin[2] at 9 a.m. on Monday, March 18.

The enclosed folder gives complete information concerning the course.

If[3] you wish to stay in campus quarters, please indicate this on the application blank. If you prefer to stay in[4] a hotel, you will need to make *your* own reservations. Accommodations in the college area are limited;[5] therefore, you should make your reservations without delay. Very truly yours, [114]

LESSON 22

187 Dear Mr. Ball: We are very glad to learn of your plans to offer a course in electronic data processing[1] next fall. We are sending you copies of the student's kit and instructor's manual that we use in our basic[2] course at Phoenix State College. We think, Mr. Ball, that you will find them helpful in planning your course.

At this time[3] we cannot give you an answer to your question about the grade level in which the course should be offered. We are[4] conducting experiments along these lines, and we should have an answer for you within the next two or three months.[5] When our report on these experiments is available, we will send you a copy.

We would like to stress that[6] the primary objective of our basic course is to interest students in the field of electronic data[7] processing, not to provide vocational competence. If we can be of further help to you, please feel free[8] to let us know. Sincerely yours, [166]

188 Dear Mr. Hunter: The odds are 10 to 1, Mr. Hunter, that Evans has the exact electronic calculator[1] you need in your office. And the odds are in your favor! Evans now offers the industry's most complete[2] line of low-cost electronic calculators. One will surely be the perfect match for any job in your office.[3]

Evans electronic printing calculators are fast with the answers and quiet in operation. The[4] printing motor runs only when activated for printing.

Why not come in soon to see our new line of calculators[5] in action. Our local office is located at 719 Fourth Street, which is across the street from the railroad[6] station. If you prefer, one of our representatives will be glad to bring several machines to your office[7] for a free demonstration. Cordially yours, [149]

189 Dear Mr. Blair: With the advent of the new 1026 Madison computer terminal, bank clerks are now[1] able to get accurate, instantaneous information about a customer's account. The new Madison[2] terminal, which was placed on the market in March, enables a bank teller to relay a transaction to[3] a central computer via a touchtone telephone and have the new balance "read" aloud to him by the computer.[4]

If you would like to see how this

terminal operates, visit our showrooms at 18 West 61[5] Street. If you would like to have one of our representatives call to give you complete information, simply indicate[6] on the enclosed card when he may call and mail it. Cordially yours, [133]

190 Dear Mr. Brown: You can cut your ordering costs with the Knight portable console ordering system. The Knight system[1] is designed to replace slow hand processing of orders with computer-fast, automatic ordering.

This[2] computer terminal is lightweight and portable and is as simple to operate as a touchtone telephone.[3] The hand-held unit weighs 24 ounces; yet it is complete with optical display so that you can check[4] your items before they are transmitted!

Whether you require hard copy, paper tape, or magnetic tape output, the[5] Knight system can satisfy your every need.

Update your ordering procedures, cut your costs, and reduce[6] ordering time from days to minutes. Write today for further information. Sincerely yours, [137]

191 Dear Mr. Ray: While I was attending a meeting in Lexington last week, I had lunch with a mutual friend of[1] ours, Harry C. Barnes. Mr. Barnes told me you had recently left the Eastern Computer Company and that you[2] are now looking for a new position.

We are organizing a West Coast sales office. If you would consider[3] moving to the West Coast, we would like to interview *you* for a position as sales representative.

If you[4] are interested, please telephone me at (213) 116-1188 to arrange for an interview.[5] Sincerely yours, [102]

LESSON 23

195 Dear Mr. Black: Your wish is our command. We tailor our computers to fit your business.

American business[1] for the past 20 years has been changing its traditional ways of operation to take advantage of the[2] exceptional benefits of the electronic computer.

Now we feel it is high time to start changing the[3] computer to accommodate the special needs of a business.

We do not, however, intend to become a custom[4] shop turning out one computer at a time. Our standard line of hardware and software is too good and too broad[5] for that.

The point is that we are going to look at business needs from a total systems point of view. We will ask,[6] "What job actually needs to be done and what is required to get the job done?" When we have the answer, we will[7] adapt our equipment to meet special needs.

Why not call us today, Mr. Black, so that we can give you more information.[8] Sincerely yours, [163]

196 Dear Mr. Jackson: Not so long ago a businessman could buy a machine that could only add and subtract. What[1] is more, he had to pay as much as $500 for it. Today for as little as $300[2] he can buy a Johnson electronic calculator that not only adds and subtracts but also multiplies³ and divides and prints out the answer. The Johnson electronic calculator is the businessman's dream.

Why not⁴ visit one of our dealers; we have 500 of them throughout the country, and no doubt there is one in your city.⁵ Or fill out and return the enclosed form, and we will send you complete information about our equipment⁶ promptly. Yours very truly, [124]

197 Dear Mr. Taylor: Thank you, Mr. Taylor, for your recent letter asking for information about the¹ qualifications necessary for a data processing teacher in a community college.

A data² processing teacher at this level should have completed a program in data processing at a recognized³ college and should have some practical business experience in data processing. In addition, he should have⁴ the usual courses in teacher education. He should also be willing to take courses every few⁵ years to bring himself up to date on the latest technological developments.

If you would like to have⁶ additional information about our data processing programs here at State College, we will be glad to send⁷ you our catalog. Sincerely yours, [145]

198 Dear Mr. Sims: Please pardon the delay in answering your letter of Friday, April 10; I have been out of¹ the office for several days and have just returned.

Here are my answers to the three questions you raised about our² teacher certification program in data processing:

1. The main objective of the program is to gain³ recognition for the profession. We do not at this time have plans to license teachers in this field.

2. We advise⁴ you to take a course in college mathematics before attempting to pass the certifying examination.⁵

3. Our experience indicates that the program appeals to people with various educational⁶ backgrounds. Some have had no college training; others have had several college degrees.

Please let me know if I⁷ can provide you with any additional information. Sincerely yours, [154]

199 Dear Mr. James: As you know, business depends on large amounts of current, accurate information. Some companies¹ write down data with pencil and paper, transcribe it into an input format, and finally forward it² to the computer operator for processing. This, of course, is slow and expensive. There is a better³ way—the Billings computer system way.

Data can be recorded at the source on a simple keyboard and transmitted⁴ over any ordinary telephone directly to a computer. This method is faster, more accurate,⁵ and much less expensive.

If you collect and use data of any kind, a Billings computer terminal⁶ can save you time and money. Sincerely yours, [129]

200 Dear Mr. Swift: As chairman of the business department of Western State College, you will be pleased to learn of our[1] new optical scanning machine that is capable of reading and scoring test answer papers. This new machine[2] will enable the members of your staff to devote more time to their students by relieving them of the tedious,[3] time-consuming job of scoring test papers.

Because of its ability to read responses and[4] simultaneously transfer the results to magnetic tape, this machine is also well suited for research in[5] compiling, sorting, and analyzing various types of data.

The machine rents for only $100[6] a month, and the time and effort saved will make it the best bargain in your school.

Mr. R. M. James, our salesman in[7] your territory, will get in touch with you in a few days to ask for an appointment to demonstrate this new[8] device. You will then be able to see for yourself the advantages of this machine. Very sincerely yours,[9]
[180]

LESSON 24

204 Dear Mr. Cohen: In data processing, any error can be costly. Fortunately, most errors can be[1] caught while programs are being carefully tested. But one type of error cannot be caught. This is the error caused[2] by defective magnetic tape.

A tape error could cost you $100, $1,000, or perhaps[3] $100,000. Such an error could cause you to lose important data forever. Then what would the[4] cost be?

We have been working on a tape that would reach you defect-free and remain defect-free. In other words, we[5] have been looking for a tape that would be extremely strong and durable.

We now have that tape—the DT 401.[6] This tape, which sells for only $20 a reel, is coated with smaller magnetic particles that can[7] be applied more evenly than ever before. The thinner coating, in turn, means a more flexible tape.

Our[8] strong tapes can make life a lot easier for you. Please let us demonstrate the DT 401 to you. Visit[9] our showrooms at 150 Sixth Avenue soon for a demonstration. We are open Monday through Friday from[10] 9 a.m. to 5 p.m.; on Saturday from 9 a.m. to 1:30 p.m. Cordially yours,   [218]

205 Dear Professor Gray: Last summer I had the pleasure of conducting a two-week seminar in data processing[1] for International Electronics. Fifty people registered for the seminar, many of whom were[2] top-management personnel. As you will see by the enclosed report, the course was so successful that International[3] Electronics has scheduled two such seminars for the coming year.

Have you given thought to a[4] similar seminar in your company? I am sure that it would be helpful to most of your employees.

If you[5] decide to conduct a seminar in data processing, I would like to apply for the position of[6] instructor. My personal data sheet is enclosed. Yours very truly,   [133]

206 Dear Dr. James: I was delighted to hear of your enjoyable, rewarding experience in teaching a[1] course in data processing at Eastern State College last summer. We have been considering such a course here at[2] Western State College, and we have definitely decided to offer it during the summer term. We are planning[3] to devote eight weeks to it.

If the course is successful, we will consider expanding our program to include[4] other data processing courses in our regular session.

Would you be interested in teaching the[5] course this summer? I would be happy to discuss the matter with you on Friday, April 6, at 10 o'clock if[6] that time is convenient for you. Sincerely yours, [129]

207 Dear Mr. Mead: Your invitation to me to teach an introductory course in data processing this summer[1] was a pleasant surprise. I am delighted to accept. In my judgment, every school of business should offer[2] at least three courses in data processing to keep abreast of the needs in today's business world. I feel that[3] the summer course will be so successful that you will definitely want to expand your course offerings in the[4] fall.

I am eager to discuss with you the possibility of a full-time position at Western State College.[5] Would Thursday, May 15, at 3 o'clock be a convenient time for me to come for an interview? If not,[6] please suggest a time that would be convenient. Sincerely yours, [130]

208 Dear Mr. James: Would you like a book that explains the principles of data processing in simple, easy-to-understand[1] language? Then *Fundamentals of Data Processing*, issued by the National Data Processing[2] Association, is the book for you.

This book is of value to the high school student, the college student, and[3] to managers who must familiarize themselves with the fundamentals of data processing. The book was[4] issued to enlighten the general reader and to increase public awareness of the importance of data processing[5] methods and equipment.

To obtain your copy, fill out the enclosed form and mail it. Upon its receipt,[6] we will send you a copy together with a bill for $12. Cordially yours, [135]

209 Dear Mr. Drake: We have been considering the installation *of* data processing equipment in our main[1] office in Denver since last April. Our volume of clerical work is growing rapidly, and we are failing[2] to meet many of our production schedules. Frankly, we need help. We know we have a problem with data, but we[3] do not know how to begin to automate our work.

Would it be possible for a representative of your[4] organization to visit us to discuss our problems? If data processing equipment will help us solve our[5] problems, we want to install it.

If you feel that you can be of help, can you come to see me next Tuesday morning[6] at 10:30? Please phone to confirm this time or to suggest another time if that is not convenient. Very[7] truly yours, [142]

LESSON 25

212 *Revolution in Office Work*

A revolution has taken place in offices across the country.

Computers and computer terminals[1] have been placed in operation in towns and cities in every state in the nation. Thousands of these "electronic[2] brains" are installed every year, representing an investment of millions of dollars.

All this means lower[3] costs, faster service, and fewer errors. It has also posed a problem. It has cut down job opportunities[4] in some types of clerical work, but it has created many new jobs of a different nature.

Shifts in[5] jobs, which are now evident, reflect just the beginning of the use of computers in the nation's business offices.[6] The first big installation took place in an insurance company in 1953. Since that time,[7] the computer has taken over a great deal of the work formerly done by armies of clerks and bookkeepers.[8]

It has become standard procedure for computers to handle jobs such as preparing payrolls, sending out bills to[9] customers, mailing checks, and maintaining the ever-increasing mass of records on employees, shareholders,[10] and customers.

Today, smaller computers and computer terminals connected to a central computer[11] are becoming available to companies that formerly could not afford the big models. At the same time,[12] all sorts of new tasks are being taken over by the machines.

In some insurance companies a computer[13] now "makes the initial decision" on whether a person qualifies for a life insurance policy. Routine[14] applications go whizzing through the machine. Those that are "out of line" are automatically shunted aside[15] for review by a well-trained, experienced underwriter.

A large California bank is using a[16] computer to review the portfolios of securities that the bank manages for its trust accounts. The[17] computer predicts returns on investments and comes up with a list of stocks and bonds that meet the standards of safety,[18] growth, income, and price established by the trust officer for each account.

A major metal company keeps[19] personnel records on magnetic tape. When jobs open up, the computer "suggests" the persons who should be considered[20] for filling them.

Chain stores and manufacturers are using computers to keep track of inventories.[21] In many firms computers now "decide" when to place orders for fresh supplies, and they even make out the order[22] slips!

Many major airlines have linked their ticket offices to a central computer. A request for a reservation[23] on any flight is relayed to the computer, which immediately assigns a seat or reports[24] back that the flight is filled.

Out of these strides in automation are coming opportunities and problems. Management[25] consultants predict that computers, in time, will lead to new lines of business not even thought of today.

In[26] the meantime, computers are enabling businesses to cut costs and

to reduce errors at the same time.[27]
[540]

213 Dear Mr. Stern: The purpose of this letter is to tell you that we have changed our name from the National Computer[1] Company to National Systems. We have made this change because we now market a wide range of data[2] processing systems, software, and services—not just computers.

In addition to delivering thousands of computer[3] terminals, we have installed hundreds of our No. 1161 data processing systems throughout[4] the world, and orders are coming in every day for this equipment. This new system is getting all kinds of[5] information into the hands of those who create and who understand and use computer results.

We would like[6] you to know more about our company and our products. Consequently, we are sending you our six-page brochure[7] that tells the full story of National Systems. Please read it; you will find it interesting. Yours very truly,[8] [160]

214 Gentlemen: The *Daily Register* has been a major factor in helping us find qualified persons for the[1] financial, accounting, and data processing openings that we had available when we started our business.[2] In fact, our advertising in the *Daily Register* helped us make our first year in business a most successful[3] one.

We will soon be opening a second office, and you may be sure that we will use the *Daily Register*[4] to help us staff it with competent people. Cordially yours, [91]

215 Dear Mr. Harris: On Monday, November 1, our bookkeeping department will be fully automated. The[1] Wilson Service Agency will handle all our billing on a computer. We are confident that this change will[2] provide our customers with faster, more efficient billing service.

We realize, of course, that during the changeover[3] there will be "bugs" in the system. Should you receive a bill that is not correct, please let us know; we will have[4] a correction made immediately.

We know that you will bear with us during the initial stages of[5] transition from hand to computer billing. Cordially yours, [110]

Chapter 6

LESSON 26

218 Dear Mr. Cunningham: We realize that you have many things to do, and the time you have left after a day's[1] work is precious. Yet we are requesting several minutes of that valuable time.

You have now had a year's[2] teaching experience, and we would like your assistance in a survey we are conducting. The purpose of the[3] survey is to determine the difficulties teachers ordinarily encounter during their first year of work.[4]

Will you please fill out the attached questionnaire and return it in the enclosed stamped, addressed envelope.

When we receive[5] all the responses to this survey, we will publish a report. If you would like to have a copy for yourself,[6] please indicate this on your questionnaire. When the report is ready, we will be happy to send a copy to[7] you.

Thank you, Mr. Cunningham, for taking the time to help us with the survey. Yours very truly,   [158]

219 Gentlemen: Will you help us serve you more efficiently? Last year we tried a new way to get to you the books you[1] needed for fall classes well before classes began. The advance-order plan was so successful that we are again[2] asking you to place your orders this spring for the books you will need in the fall. This plan, which helps us schedule[3] our production more effectively, eliminates the usual last-minute rush to get all books to the[4] schools by the beginning of the fall term.

The advance-order plan offers you the following significant[5] advantages:

1. It enables you to receive, check, and store your books well before the beginning of classes in[6] September.

2. It gives teachers time to look over their new books at their leisure and to prepare for their fall classes.[7]

3. It gives you the opportunity to receive your books early but pay for them in September as[8] usual.

Please help us help you; use our advance-order plan. An order blank is enclosed for your convenience. Yours[9] truly,   [181]

220 Dear Dr. Clark: As a result of the growth of our career education department, we are planning to expand[1] our present program. We are going to add a number of courses and install an office-simulation[2] laboratory.

Before equipping this laboratory, we would like to have your opinion concerning the business[3] machines we should purchase. Will it be possible for you to visit our campus during the last week of June?[4]

We will appreciate any suggestions you make. Sincerely yours, [93]

221 Dear Mr. Gray: As chairman of the chemistry section of the science teachers convention, it is my pleasant[1] duty to obtain a speaker for our annual meeting. You have been recommended as a possible speaker[2] by Mr. Carl Teller, president of the Atlantic Chemical Company. Mr. Teller writes me that[3] you could make a significant contribution to our program.

The convention will be held on Friday, February[4] 6. The sectional meetings, including ours in chemistry, will start at 2 o'clock and run for two[5] hours.

As I must send a copy of our program to the printer by December 15, please let me know as soon[6] as possible whether you can accept this invitation. Yours very truly,   [134]

222 Dear Mr. Smith: As I am sure you realize, more than 90 percent of the country's private schools must rely[1] on contributions from friends, alumni, and parents of students to balance their budgets. Wilson Academy[2] is one of them.

This year Wilson Academy must raise $55,000 from contributions to[3] balance the budget. Of this amount, we have collected $47,000 as of August 1. We[4] still have a few weeks to raise the $8,000 necessary to reach our goal.

We would be most grateful for[5] any contribution you care to make. Won't you write a check for the Wilson Academy Fund and mail it in[6] the enclosed envelope. Sincerely yours, [125]

223 Dear Mr. Decker: Yesterday I learned from one of my professors that the government offers college graduates[1] of schools of business administration an opportunity to apply for scholarships in foreign countries.[2]

I am very much interested in studying in France or Spain. Would you please send me whatever information[3] and forms I need to fill out to apply.

I understand that these applications must be filed by November[4] 1; consequently, I would appreciate it if you would send me the forms as soon as possible. Yours truly,[5] [100]

224 Dear Mr. West: I am enclosing a booklet that explains the scholarships that the government offers college[1] graduates of schools of business administration. I am also enclosing the forms you must fill out.

To be[2] eligible for one of these scholarships, you must file your application by November 1. Sincerely yours,[3] [80]

225 Dear Miss Wilson: It is a pleasure to accept your invitation to speak at your meeting on Friday, February[1] 6. When you know the exact time and place of your meeting, please let me know.

Since you did not specify a[2] subject for my talk, I assume that you are leaving the choice to me. May I suggest "New Trends in Education"[3] as my topic. If you consider this too broad an area to cover in an hour's talk, please suggest some other[4] topic.

I am looking forward to visiting with you and the teachers in your district in February.[5] Cordially yours, [102]

LESSON 27

230 Dear Mr. Spencer: Now that you will be graduating from high school in a few months, you are surely thinking about[1] college. We hope that you will consider Harrisburg College as the institution in which to continue[2] your education.

There are, of course, many types of colleges, and you should investigate several colleges[3] carefully before you choose the one you will attend.

Harrisburg College, which is a small liberal arts[4] school, has an outstanding academic record. As you will see by studying our offerings in the enclosed catalog,[5] we give our students a complete, well-rounded education.

If you would like to visit Harrisburg to[6] see our campus, please let us know; we will arrange for one of our counselors to be your host. Sincerely yours,[7] [140]

231 To the Staff: Last fall we conducted a survey among our students to determine what type of school year they would[1] prefer. The students overwhelmingly chose the quarter system. The administration of the American[2] Institute has decided, therefore, to drop the two-semester system and substitute the quarter system to[3] go into effect next year.

No doubt you are very much interested in the implications of this change in[4] your own program. Consequently, I am calling a meeting of the faculty on Friday, June 15, at 4[5] o'clock at which time this change will be discussed.

Please make every effort to be present. R. C. Bates   [118]

232 Dear Mr. Jones: Your description of Plattsburg Junior College is very appealing. It seems to be the type of[1] college I would like to attend.

Please send me the necessary forms to make application for admission.

I[2] would like to visit the campus on Saturday, June 15. Please let me know if this day is convenient for you.[3] Sincerely yours,   [62]

233 Dear Mr. Jones: Enclosed is our catalog and an application blank for enrollment in the Pittsburgh College[1] of Commerce. If you wish to apply for the fall term, fill out and return this blank as soon as possible.

The tuition[2] committee recently recommended a new schedule of fees, and this schedule was adopted by the[3] board of trustees. A list of the new rates is attached to the catalog.

If you choose to come to the Pittsburgh[4] College of Commerce, we are sure you will find our programs interesting, challenging, and rewarding. We hope to receive[5] your application soon. Cordially yours, [108]

234 Dear Professor Burns: This summer we are planning to expand our course offerings at the Central College of[1] Canada in the field of art education. You have been recommended to us as a well-qualified teacher[2] in this field. We would, therefore, like to offer you a position as a visiting lecturer during the summer[3] term.

We plan to offer an eight-week course, a four-week course, and a two-day seminar. At the present time, we need[4] three teachers for these courses.

Will you please let me know before February 15 if you are interested[5] in teaching at the Central College of Canada this summer. If you are, I am sure that we will be able[6] to reach a satisfactory agreement on salary.

I hope that you can be with us, Professor Burns; you[7] will find Halifax a delightful place to spend your summer. Sincerely yours,   [154]

235 Dear Mr. Weber: It is with a great deal of pleasure that I accept your offer to teach in the summer program[1] of the Central College of Canada. If you can arrange it, I would prefer to teach a course *in* art history.[2] However, any area of art education will be satisfactory.

May I ask your[3] assistance in helping me find a house in Halifax for the months of June and July.

I have always considered[4] your school one of the finest in Canada; therefore, I am delighted to have the opportunity to join[5] your faculty next summer. Sincerely yours,   [108]

LESSON 28

239 Dear Professor Smith: After teaching language courses at the South Side Grammar School in Phoenix for the past two years,[1] I have decided to continue my education on the graduate level. Your college, I understand,[2] has graduate programs in both French and Spanish education, and I would like information concerning[3] the degree requirements for these fields.

My undergraduate degree in Spanish is from State College. I have[4] had teaching experience in French, Spanish, and German.

Will you please send me information concerning your program[5] as soon as possible as I would like to register for courses beginning this summer. Very sincerely[6] yours, [121]

240 Dear Mr. Rice: Dr. John Andrews, director of our foreign language program, is interested in recruiting[1] students who would like to become language teachers. Therefore, he would welcome an invitation to speak to the[2] seniors of your high school.

Dr. Andrews will be visiting several high schools in your area during the[3] next few weeks. In his talks he presents the many opportunities available to students who are prepared[4] to teach foreign languages. He emphasizes that learning a foreign language prepares the student for teaching[5] as well as for a variety of other positions in international business.

If you would like Dr.[6] Andrews to talk to your seniors, just indicate on the enclosed card the day that would be most convenient for[7] him to come. The card requires no postage. Sincerely yours,   [150]

241 Dear Mr. Ryan: Thank you for your gracious offer to have Dr. Andrews talk to our seniors on the opportunities[1] in the foreign language field. I suggest 2:30 p.m. on Wednesday, March 3, as the most convenient[2] time for us to have Dr. Andrews on campus. We have about 30 students who are interested in[3] this field, and they will be eager to hear Dr. Andrews' talk.

We look forward to hearing from you. Sincerely yours,[4]   [80]

242 Dear Mr. Johnson: As you requested, we are sending you a bulletin describing the courses offered in[1] our School of Business. We have major programs in management, accounting, finance, and general business.

The School[2] of Business was organized in 1912, and during our years of operation, we have established a[3] reputation as one of the most progressive, forward-looking schools in the nation.

We would appreciate it if[4] you would discuss our bulletin with the seniors in your high school. In a few days our representative, Mr.[5] Harold

Atkins, will call at your school to talk with any students who are interested in attending the School[6] of Business.

If you have any questions, please feel free to write us. Yours very truly, [135]

243 Dear Miss Hunt: You will be happy to know that your application to reside in Baker Hall, our newest dormitory,[1] has been accepted.

The residence halls will open on Saturday, September 14. Classes will begin[2] on Monday, September 16.

The girls are expected to furnish their own linens, towels, and blankets for[3] their rooms. Most electrical appliances are not permitted. If you wish, however, you may bring a small electric[4] coffeepot.

When you bring your baggage to the dormitory, please use the entrance on the Fourth Avenue[5] side.

We are looking forward to having you with us this coming school year. Very sincerely yours, [117]

244 Dear Congressman Martin: Many thanks for your participation in the January 15 meeting of our[1] staff. You have given us many ideas that I know will be of great help to us in preparing materials[2] that will meet the needs of children living in urban areas.

Our check covering your honorarium[3] and expenses is enclosed.

Once again, please accept our sincere thanks for taking time from your busy day to be[4] with us. Sincerely yours, [84]

245 Dear Mrs. Anderson: Thank you for your letter *of* July 2 requesting information about our master's[1] degree program in business. As every student's program is designed individually, I cannot list[2] *the* specific courses you would be required to take. In general, though, I can say that the program is divided[3] between regular business and liberal arts courses.

I am sending you separately our *Graduate Bulletin.*[4] I hope, Mrs. Anderson, that this information will be helpful to you. Sincerely yours, [97]

LESSON 29

249 Dear Mr. Williams: Before you sign a new contract this spring, you may want to consider the possibility[1] of teaching in another part of the country. Why not let us help you find a new position. We have helped[2] thousands of teachers obtain the jobs that are suited to their individual qualifications in areas[3] where they wish to live.

We will have a number of vacancies for elementary school teachers in all parts of[4] the country next fall. On the secondary level, except in a few specialized subjects, you will find strong[5] competition; consequently, our experience will be very valuable to you.

An application blank[6] is enclosed for your convenience in registering with us. Do not delay; fill out the form and return it now.[7] Sincerely yours, [142]

250 Dear Mr. Bates: Our faculty committee met yesterday to select those students who will receive graduate[1] fellowships for the coming year, and it is my privilege to tell you that you have been awarded a research[2] fellowship in the science department. This fellowship will pay you $500 a month for the nine months[3] of the school year. You will be working with your major professor, Dr. Paul Jones.

The project that you proposed has[4] been approved by the research committee for both the fellowship and for thesis credit.

You have my congratulations[5] and best wishes, Mr. Bates, for a stimulating, productive year of study. Cordially yours, [119]

251 Dear Professor Gray: Thank you for your letter telling me that I have been awarded a research fellowship for[1] the coming school year.

I was very happy to learn that the project has also been approved for my thesis. As[2] you know, Dr. Jones and I have been doing preliminary work on this project, and it is rewarding to[3] know that our plans have now been approved. I am looking forward to the opportunity of working full time on[4] my thesis, and I sincerely appreciate the financial assistance that the fellowship will provide. Sincerely[5] yours, [101]

252 Dear Mrs. Mann: To assist your high school class in a study of telephone courtesy, we are sending you[1] separately several booklets on the subject. Please accept them with our compliments.

Last year we issued two films that[2] should also be of interest to your class. The films are entitled *Proper Telephone Techniques* and *Telephone[3] Courtesy*. The first deals with the technical aspects of telephone usage; the other deals with human relationships.[4] If you would like to use either of these films, we will be glad to make them available to you free of[5] charge.

Our school representative, Miss Jane Johnson, can arrange to show the films to your class and answer any questions[6] the students might have. She will bring all the necessary equipment when she comes to your school.

Please telephone[7] Miss Johnson at 687-8101 if you would like her to visit your school. Sincerely yours, [158]

253 Dear Miss Long: The National Steamship Company would like to invite your office practice class to make a one-hour[1] informal tour of its modern, well-equipped offices any Monday or Friday between the hours of 8:30[2] a.m. and 4 p.m. During the tour your students will have an opportunity to see all the functions[3] of our office. Afterwards, they will have an opportunity to ask any questions they may have about our[4] procedures, equipment, and personnel.

If you wish to accept this invitation, please call me at 451-4111;[5] I will be happy to arrange the tour for you. Yours very truly, [115]

254 Dear Mr. Farmington: Thank you for your kind invitation to the office practice class of our high school to visit[1] your organization. We are delighted *to* accept.

The class is especially interested in seeing[2] your calculators, computers, and duplicators in operation. After a trip through well-equipped, modern[3] offices such as yours, our class discussions will be more stimulating and meaningful.

Friday, February[4] 13, at 2 p.m. will be the most convenient time for us. If that date and time are inconvenient, please[5] call me at 116-1117 any time *between* 8 a.m. and 3 p.m.

Sincerely yours,   [118]

LESSON 30

257 *The Stock Market*

A stock market is simply a place where buyers and sellers of shares in a corporation can get together[1] to conduct business. Large corporations can sell stocks and bonds there to raise the money they need to expand. People[2] with savings to invest can quickly and easily put their money to work in private investments. Such investments[3] may earn money for investors and enable industries to grow.

Bonds are basically loans to companies.[4] They earn a set rate of interest which must be paid by the borrower even if the company does not[5] make a profit. Bondholders do not share in profits and have no voice in company management.

Shares of stock,[6] however, represent ownership in the business and give the shareholder the right to vote for company directors.[7] If the business is profitable, stockholders will probably receive dividends—a percentage of the[8] company's profits. For example, if you buy 10 shares of a corporation's stock at $20 a share,[9] you own $200 worth of the stock. If the corporation declares a dividend of $1 a share[10] for the year, you receive $10 in dividends.

Many people buy stock because they hope to realize a[11] higher rate of income through dividends than their savings can earn in a savings account at a bank. Others hope[12] their stock will rise in price so that they can make a capital gain. For example, if the market price of your 10[13] shares of stock went up to $25 a share, you would realize a $50 capital gain. The[14] ideal situation is to buy stock when the price is low and sell when the price is high. As most investors know,[15] however, that is not easy.

The long-term trend in stock prices, however, is up. Thus experts advise that anyone[16] who buys a reasonably good selection of stocks should find his investment increasing in value over[17] a period of time.

What makes the price of a stock go up and down? Find the answer to that question and you[18] are likely to make a fortune! There are, however, a number of factors that can influence prices at which[19] stocks sell.

First is the profit outlook. When a corporation is making good profits and the future looks bright, its[20] stock will be in demand. Thus buyers are likely to "bid up" the price. Conversely, when a company is losing[21] money and its future is questionable, the stock is not likely to be in demand and the price is likely[22] to fall. Thus experts caution buyers to study a company's financial record before buying its stock.

Second[23] is the economy. When the overall national economy is prosperous, business is prosperous,[24] and the stock market usually moves higher. When the economy is in a recession, stock prices[25] usually fall. Some people believe that the stock market influences the health of the economy. Many[26] experts feel, however, that the market is an indicator of business conditions rather than a cause.[27]

Third is rumors. News, whether it is true or not, can have a great impact on individual stock prices. If,[28] for instance, word got around that an oil company has made some fabulous oil strike or that a company was[29] about to market an important new moneymaking product or device, many investors would scramble to[30] buy the stock, thus "bidding up" the price. A negative rumor could have the opposite effect.

At times a great many[31] stockholders may decide during the same period that it is a good time to buy stocks. When enough buyers[32] do so and the total market begins to rise, the rising market is called a "bull" market. When the general[33] trend is to sell stocks, causing a declining market, this is called a "bear" market.

It takes patience and ingenuity[34] to tell with any accuracy when the market will be bullish or bearish— or why it is either.[35] Most financial experts can tell you why the market has had a good or bad year. But ask them which way the market[36] will turn next, and you have asked a ringer. [727]—Adapted from "Investment: The Lure of Wall Street," *Senior Scholastic,* May 9, 1968, pp. 14-16.

258 Dear Miss Green: Today hundreds of women are enjoying satisfying careers in our service organization.[1] The reason is simple: Our technical representatives must have the poise, tact, and understanding to be[2] vital links between our company and our customers. They must have the ability to work efficiently[3] and independently. Women possess these talents as well as men.

If you have a high school diploma or its[4] equivalent and a good understanding of basic electronics, you may qualify as a trainee at[5] full pay. In a short time you will be assigned your own territory in the area in which you live. You will[6] enjoy a good salary and an outstanding program of fringe benefits that includes profit sharing.

If you[7] believe you qualify, call Mr. A. C. Smith, our personnel manager, for an appointment. His number is[8] 116-1818, Extension 118. Yours very truly, [173]

Chapter 7

LESSON 31

261 Dear Mr. Brown: Your request for information regarding the convention of the National Manufacturers[1] Association has been referred to me. It is a pleasure to supply the information you request.[2]

The National Manufacturers Association will hold its convention at the Western Hotel beginning[3] on Monday, August 15. If you wish to exhibit your merchandise at this convention, you should write Mr.[4] James Green, who is the exhibit chairman for the organization. Mr. Green will be glad to tell you what[5] booths are available and the price of each. Very truly yours, [112]

262 Dear Mr. Green: Mr. Jack Simms has written us that you are the exhibit chairman for the convention of the[1] National Manufacturers Association.

Our company would like to exhibit its new, low-cost line[2] of merchandise at this meeting if space is still available. Will you please send us information on the booths[3] available and the rental charges. Sincerely yours, [70]

263 Dear Mr. Brown: Enclosed is a list of the exhibit booths still available for the convention of the National Manufacturers[1] Association. We have several single booths and one double booth that have not yet been assigned.[2] The rental charge for the single booths is $100. The double booth, because of its favorable location,[3] is $300.

Requests for space are coming in daily; therefore, we suggest that you make your[4] reservation as soon as possible. Sincerely yours, [90]

264 Dear Mrs. Moore: It is a pleasure for us to write you that the Turner Hotel has been selected as the[1] headquarters of the Eastern Horse Show to be held in Providence on September 18.

At the request of Mr.[2] R. R. Myers, chairman of the hospitality committee, we are setting aside a block of 15 rooms[3] for exhibitors. As you will see by the enclosed reservation card, we are offering these rooms at the special[4] exhibitor's rate of $18 a day.

If you plan to attend this show, please make your reservation[5] early. Very truly yours, [104]

265 Dear Mr. Harris: It is a pleasure for me, on behalf of the Hotel Association of Chicago,[1] to extend a cordial invitation to the Central Medical Association to hold its annual convention[2] in Chicago next year.

Our city is fortunate in having ample facilities to take care of[3] the needs of even the largest organizations in the country. Furthermore, Chicago is easily[4] accessible by all means of transportation. Our location at the nation's crossroads attracts hundreds of conventions[5] annually.

We would like to invite you and the other officers of the association to Chicago[6] as our guests to see the facilities that we have available.

Please call me collect to make arrangements[7] for your trip to Chicago. It will be a pleasure to be your host. Sincerely yours, [156]

266 Dear Mr. Simmons: From all appearances, we are going to have a capacity crowd at the Baker Hotel[1] this winter.

Since it is our desire to accommodate all our friends at the times that best suit them, we would[2] appreciate your advising us of the exact dates of your intended visit. Also, we would appreciate[3] your sending us the customary deposit of $50.

It would be a great help if you could let us[4] have this information within the next ten days. Very truly yours, [93]

267 Dear Miss Davis: Nothing would please us more than to serve as the headquarters of the convention of the National[1] Chemical Association during the week of October 10. We are grateful for this opportunity[2] to tell you all about our facilities.

We have two air-conditioned meeting rooms that should be completely adequate[3] to take care of the needs of your organization. Each room seats 150 people and is equipped[4] with a screen, movie projector, and overhead projector.

Your members will enjoy our three dining rooms[5] in which we serve the finest foods at reasonable prices.

May I invite you, Miss Davis, to come in soon and[6] see for yourself how well we are equipped to serve you. Would it be possible for you to have lunch with me one day[7] next week? Call me at 415-6118, and we can select a day that will be mutually convenient.[8] Yours very truly, [164]

268 Dear Mrs. Ford: It has been a year since we have had an opportunity to serve you at the Palm Hotel, but[1] we have not forgotten you. Nothing would please us more, Mrs. Ford, than to have you spend your vacation with us.

The[2] Palm Hotel has a world-famous reputation for providing the best in facilities, food, and service.

The[3] same experienced staff that served you last year is *ready** to serve you again.

A reservation card is enclosed[4] for your convenience. We promise you that your vacation with us will be a memorable one. Very truly[5] yours, [101]

Also correct:
*eager, waiting

LESSON 32

273 Dear Mr. Hanley: No doubt you will soon be making plans for the annual convention of the American[1] Insurance Association in Philadelphia. You will, of course, have to decide which hotel to make your[2] headquarters. May we invite you to consider the Hotel Ford for this purpose.

Because of the extensive[3] remodeling we have done during the past three or four months, we are in a position to provide your members with[4] the finest, most modern facilities.

Your members will also be pleased

with the special low room and suite rates that[5] we give to groups such as yours.

Our meeting rooms should be more than adequate to accommodate your needs; they are[6] available for your use without extra charge.

We will be glad to have you visit us as our guest, Mr. Hanley,[7] at any time that will suit your convenience. During your visit you will be able to see the complete,[8] well-planned facilities that will be at the disposal of your members. Sincerely yours, [176]

274   Dear Mr. Glass: As your records will show, my family and I occupied a suite at the Salem Hotel from[1] March 11 through 16. I sent a check for $25 as a deposit in February.[2] When I checked out on March 16, I paid the bill of $200.

I should have verified the charges when[3] we left but, in the hurry of leaving, I did not do so. It occurred to me that I may have overpaid our[4] bill by $25. Will you please look into this matter for me.

We enjoyed our stay at your hotel very[5] much. The service was superb, and the courtesy of the hotel employees contributed to making our[6] stay particularly pleasant. Yours very truly, [130]

275   Dear Mr. Frank: It was indeed a pleasure to have had you and your family as guests at the Salem Hotel;[1] we hope that you will plan to return in the near future.

Enclosed is a copy of your account showing the charges[2] that we made during the week of March 11.

You will observe that we did deduct the $25[3] deposit from your account; the total bill was $225 before the deduction.

We look[4] forward to having you as guests at our hotel again soon. Sincerely yours, [93]

276   Dear Mr. Weber: Arrangements are almost complete for your business meeting and banquet to be held on January[1] 27 in the Grand Hall of the Hotel Dover. A copy of the dinner menu is enclosed.[2] Will you please return it by Friday, January 20, indicating any changes you would like to make.

We[3] suggest that you let us have a minimum of an hour and a half to prepare this room for your banquet. If you[4] wish to have dinner served at 6:30, you should plan to complete your business meeting by 5 o'clock.

As you request,[5] we will place a grand piano near the head table before the banquet.

If we can be of any further[6] assistance to you in arranging your meeting at the Dover, please let us know. Yours very truly, [138]

277   Dear Mr. Willis: I have just learned that during the week of June 18, we had the privilege of extending to[1] you the hospitality of the Hotel West. I hope that your stay was a most enjoyable one and that you[2] will consider it your home whenever you are in Milwaukee on business or pleasure.

We are always on the lookout[3] for ways to improve our service to our guests. That is why we ask each guest to fill out the enclosed questionnaire.[4] Won't you do this for us? Also, please let us have any suggestions on services that are not included in[5] the questionnaire. An envelope is also enclosed for your convenience.

Thank you, Mr. Willis, for the privilege[6] of serving you. Yours very truly,   [127]

278   Dear Mr. Burns: The arrangements committee of the Pennsylvania Football Coaches Association is in[1] the process of deciding on a hotel in which to hold its annual convention in Philadelphia[2] on August 10, 11, and 12. The Hotel Benson has been *suggested** as a possible site.

Do you extend[3] the courtesy of complimentary rooms to committees reviewing facilities for consideration[4] of a convention site? If you do, three officers of the association would like to come to the Benson on[5] Saturday, May 10, to see your facilities.

We look forward to hearing from you soon. Sincerely yours,[6]   [120]
Also correct:
**mentioned, recommended

LESSON 33

282   Gentlemen: When I checked out of the Peerless Hotel on Friday night, March 16, I thoughtlessly left the following[1] articles in Room 116:
1. A small camera
2. Three blue shirts
3. A package containing two books[2]
If these articles have been turned in to your lost and found department, I would appreciate your sending them to[3] me by parcel post. Needless to say, I will be glad to pay all handling charges. Sincerely yours,   [77]

283   Dear Mr. Green: On Friday, February 1, the new Dawson Hotel will open its doors for the first time. This[1] new hotel, located in the heart of Cleveland, has been designed for today's traveling public. Large, well-equipped[2] rooms and fine restaurants will make your stay enjoyable. Whether you come to Cleveland by car or plane, you will find[3] the Dawson a convenient, friendly place to stay.

If you drive, you will be able to leave your car in our garage[4] free of charge. One of our courteous attendants will be glad to park it for you and have it ready for you when[5] you need it. If you arrive by plane, the Dawson bus will meet your flight and take you right to the front door of the hotel.[6]

For the utmost in comfort and service, stay at the Dawson the next time business takes you to Cleveland. Cordially[7] yours,   [141]

284   Dear Mr. Burns: As you no doubt noticed on your visit to our hotel last week, we are making major improvements[1] in our dining room facilities. The work is progressing nicely, but we realize that we cannot give[2] our guests the type of service that they have learned to expect from our staff.

When the work is completed, the capacity[3] of our main dining room will be more than doubled. The coffee shop, too, will be larger and more comfortable.[4]

We hope that by the time you

visit us again, all the work will have been completed and our staff will once again[5] be able to render you the service that has made the Wilson one of Chicago's leading hotels.

In the meantime,[6] thank you for your patience. Yours very truly, [129]

285 Dear Mr. Deems: At 42 East Washington Street in uptown Indianapolis, you will find a new hotel,[1] the Wellington, a hotel unlike any you have visited before.

It is designed especially for[2] you, the salesman who travels by car. Upon your arrival and check-in, you can carry your own luggage to your[3] room if you wish. If you want a porter to take care of your luggage, one will be readily available.

You[4] will be able to park your car yourself in our garage. You will be assigned a spacious, climate-controlled room. Best[5] of all, you will like our rates; they are the lowest of any major hotel in the city.

The Wellington is[6] located in the heart of the business district and is convenient to all major business buildings.

As manager[7] of the Wellington, I invite you to stay with us the next time you are in Indianapolis. Sincerely[8] yours, [161]

286 Gentlemen: Please reserve a single room for me for April 1, 2, and 3. I will be driving to Akron to[1] attend the American Management Association convention and will arrive about 5 p.m.[2] on April 1. However, just in case my arrival is delayed, I would like to guarantee

the room. Enclosed[3] is a check for $20 for this purpose.

Please confirm my reservation. Sincerely yours, [77]

287 Dear Mr. Budd: The Mason Hotel in New York has more to offer than any other hotel in the city.[1] It is located in midtown and is close to everything you want to see and do in New York.

Staying at[2] the Mason Hotel is easy on your budget. For as little as $18 a day you can have a fine[3] room with radio and television.

So the next time you are in New York on business or pleasure, come to the[4] Mason.

For reservations, call us at (415) 216-1881. Yours truly, [97]

288 Gentlemen: The Seattle Secretaries Institute would like to reserve several rooms at the Hotel Wilson[1] for its annual meeting on February 11, 12, and 13. Three connecting rooms would *suit*° our[2] needs ideally. We will need these rooms from 8 a.m. to 5 p.m. each day.

In each room we will need a chalkboard,[3] an overhead projector, and a lectern.

If you can accommodate us on these days, please let me know as soon[4] as possible. Sincerely yours, [86]

Also correct:
°fit, meet, take care of

LESSON 34

292 Dear Mr. Collins: Almost anywhere your business takes you, you can enjoy the convenience of a Continental[1] Motel. Continental understands what a businessman wants from a motel, and it endeavors to give it[2] to him.

Continental Motels are located in the large business cities of the world and in the small ones, too.[3] A Continental Motel is ideal for business meetings and conventions. We keep you on top of things where[4] the action is; however, we don't forget the small attentions that let you relax, enjoy a good dinner, and[5] have an undisturbed night's sleep.

Whenever you travel on business, (400) 134-2593 is the[6] one number that makes your trip enjoyable. Call this number any time, day or night, to reserve a room at any[7] Continental Motel. Very truly yours,   [149]

293 Dear Mr. James: It is with great pride that we announce the opening on Saturday, December 10, of the Western[1] Hotel, one of the most elegant hotels in the world. It is the height of luxury, towering 25[2] stories over Central Park in the heart of San Francisco.

Our 3,000 spacious, nicely furnished guest rooms[3] and suites are air conditioned and equipped with radio and color television.

We know you will enjoy the[4] many extras our hotel offers, including a gymnasium, sauna, and swimming pool. Parking is free, of[5] course, for all our guests.

Three magnificent restaurants cater to the most discriminating appetite. One restaurant,[6] The Quick

Chef, is open 24 hours a day for a sandwich or a complete meal.

When you want the ultimate[7] in hotel accommodations in San Francisco, come to the Western. Cordially yours,   [157]

294 Dear Mr. Harris: We were sorry to learn from your letter that you do not have three single rooms available[1] at the Hotel Jennings for March 12 and 13. As you suggested, we will accept one double room and one single[2] room. If, however, there are cancellations before our arrival, please reserve three single rooms for us. Sincerely[3] yours,   [62]

295 Dear Mr. Jackson: You will be happy to know that we have had cancellations of reservations for several[1] single rooms for March 12 and 13 and that we are now able to reserve three single rooms for you and your[2] party for those evenings.

The rate for each of the rooms is $20 a day. We will hold the rooms until[3] 6 p.m. on March 12, unless you care to guarantee payment by sending us your check for $60.

We[4] are looking forward to having you at our hotel. Cordially yours,   [93]

296 Dear Miss Billings: This will confirm our telephone conversation of Friday, October 12, in which you reserved[1] the Albany Hotel's Lake View Room for a luncheon to be held on November 10 from 12 noon until 2 p.m.[2]

Enclosed are copies of our luncheon menus. Will you please check the menu that you prefer and return it to[3] us by November 1. We will also need to know by November 8 the number of people you expect to[4] attend your meeting.

We are sure that you will enjoy the fine service and the high-quality food at the Lake View[5] Room. We are looking forward to having your group with us. Cordially yours, [113]

297 Dear Mr. Jackson: When a businessman visits Chicago, he has a large choice of hotels and motels at which[1] he can stay.

Most of the hotels and motels, of course, advertise comfortable rooms, prompt service, and reasonable[2] rates. However, do they offer:

1. Free parking?
2. Color television in each room?
3. One-day laundry[3] service seven days a week?

Those are a few of the special services that will be at your disposal when you[4] stay at the Reagan Hotel.

The next time your business takes you to Chicago, why not stay with us. Tell us at which[5] airport you will arrive and what time you will arrive. We will have transportation ready to take you to the[6] Reagan— at no cost to you.

We guarantee you a visit that you will long remember. Very truly yours,

P.S.[7] To make reservations, call us collect at (116) 118-2222. [155]

298 Dear Mr. James: The Convention Bureau of Los Angeles extends a friendly invitation to you to hold[1] the annual convention of the West-

ern Press Association in our city next year.

Los Angeles has[2] been called the ideal convention city, and after you have held your convention here, we think you will agree[3] that this description is accurate. We are *confident,** Mr. James, that your membership will enjoy the many[4] advantages of meeting here. As you know, Los Angeles is easily accessible by several major[5] airlines.

We hope that Los Angeles will have the privilege of extending to the Western Press Association[6] a sincere welcome at its convention next year. Yours very truly, [134]
Also correct:
*sure, certain

LESSON 35

301 *The Motel Business*

Tourist cabins, the forerunners of the motel, paralleled the development of extensive travel by[1] automobile in the late 1920's. These early cabins were a far cry from the present-day deluxe motel.[2] The tourist cabins did have convenience of location. They were near the highway and usually at the edge[3] of a town or city. The cabin provided the traveler a convenient place to relax and a place to[4] park his car near the cabin door. This early forerunner of the motel provided limited facilities[5] and represented Spartan living at best. There was no central heating, and the bathhouse was often located[6] in a central building which served all the units in the cluster of cabins. The traveler usually had[7] to stand in line for his "hot" shower.

The term *motel* was first used in the 1930's, and the word was formed by[8] combining part of the words *motor* and *hotel*. The early motels often were family-owned businesses located[9] along the roads leading to vacation areas. They relied mainly on tourist traffic and offered[10] merely a place for the motorist to rest. They had no television, no swimming pool, and usually no[11] restaurant. The factors of convenience of location and a place to park the car nearby were the basis on[12] which the motel industry developed. Since these small enterprises operated at a profit, it soon became[13] evident that the motel business could develop into a major industry.

With the investment of[14] capital by large organizations came the deluxe motel with additional facilities. Swimming pools[15] and television sets became as essential to a motel as parking areas. Additional services[16] such as bowling alleys, playgrounds, and baby-sitters are now provided by many motels. In some states,[17] air-conditioned kennels are provided for the motel guest who brings his dog with him.

The convenience of parking one's[18] car in front of the motel room is sometimes provided at great expense. A few of the large, multistory motels[19] provide parking accommodations in front of the room even though that room may be on the twentieth floor![20] An elevator actually lifts the car to the proper floor and parks it in front of the guest room.

In the[21] early days motels were not owned or operated by major hotel corporations. However, as the motel[22] business boomed and the occupancy rate in hotels dropped, the hotel chains began to invest in motels. Now[23] many of the hotel chains also operate numerous motels.

Motels are now also located near air terminals[24] for the convenience of the air traveler. It is interesting to note that they are still often called[25] "motels." One use of the air terminal motel is to provide conference facilities for companies that[26] bring executives together from various parts of the country for a meeting. Such conferences are frequently[27] known as "fly-in" meetings.

The development of the luxury motel, with added conveniences for[28] the traveler, has resulted in increased room rates. Sometimes the deluxe, but expensive, conveniences are not[29] wanted or appreciated by the travelers. The guest who arrives at a motel late at night and leaves early[30] the following morning often pays a room rate that includes many conveniences he had no opportunity[31] to utilize. As he leaves, he may have a feeling of disappointment and frustration that he has paid[32] for, but not used, the swimming pool, the color television set, or the golf course.

The concept on which the original[33] motel was developed was to provide a convenient stopping place for the tourist and to assure him[34] of a comfortable place to get a good night's sleep—and little more. For the traveler who arrives late at night[35] and leaves early the next morning, the original idea of an inexpensive, but conveniently located,[36] facility may be exactly what he wishes.

To meet the needs of the traveler who does not have[37] time to enjoy the luxuries that go with the deluxe motel, there are now several economy motel[38] chains which have built units throughout the country. The average room in the economy motel is small, and the[39] facilities are limited. But the economy motel does provide the comforts necessary for a[40] good night's sleep at a much lower rate than the deluxe motel. Therefore, the traveler today can select the type[41] of motel that best fits his time and budget.   [827]

Chapter 8

LESSON 36

304 Gentlemen: Your records will show that in 1966 I purchased life insurance policy No.[1] 16151 and that I have paid the premiums on this policy regularly.

I now find it imperative[2] to review my entire insurance program. May I request you, therefore, to do the following for me:[3]

1. Determine the present cash value of this policy.

2. Have one of your representatives call me to[4] arrange an appointment to discuss my complete insurance program.

If you will have your agent call me at[5] 415-1515 between 9 a.m. and 5 p.m. on any weekday, we can arrange an appointment for[6] a convenient time. Very truly yours, [127]

305 Dear Mr. Mason: Some time ago I asked ten of my friends to name the companies with which they carry fire,[1] accident, and liability insurance. Only one could do so! Nine of them said, "I can't."

Many businessmen[2] buy their insurance blindfolded; they do not bother to learn the name of the insurance company. Would you[3] ever buy a car—or even a cigar—that way?

Your insurance, which is worth thousands of dollars to you, could[4] be the only thing between you and financial catastrophe. It is important, therefore, to know who is promising[5] to pay you if you have a loss. You should be sure that the company you select is strong and safe under all[6] circumstances.

Why not let a representative of the National Insurance Company, one of the largest[7] in the world, visit you to discuss our programs with you. His call will place you under no obligation.

Know[8] your insurance company, and put your mind at ease. Sincerely yours,   [173]

306 Dear Mr. Baker: At what price would you sell your manufacturing plant tomorrow? This question would probably[1] be a difficult one for you to answer on the spur of the moment.

Loss of your plant facilities,

whether[2] total or partial, is like an involuntary sale. When you receive a check in settlement of a loss, you[3] have actually "sold" the destroyed property to the insurance company.

Do you have sufficient insurance[4] coverage to take care of replacement costs if such a "sale" becomes necessary? With property values at[5] an all-time high, it is urgent for you to have an answer to this question.

I would like to discuss with you a[6] plan that could save you many times its cost by giving you vital facts about your property. Return the enclosed[7] postage-paid card to arrange an interview; you will never regret doing so. Very truly yours, [158]

307 Gentlemen: The business of the World Insurance Company has grown to such an extent during the past few years[1] that we are planning to establish a branch office in Chicago.

We are looking for a responsible, progressive[2] young person to represent us in this territory. It occurred to us that you might know of someone[3] who would be interested in this position.

The person we need should have the following qualifications:

1.[4] He must have a keen interest in the insurance business.

2. He must be a college graduate.

3. He must[5] have had at least three years' successful experience in the insurance business.

If your employment agency[6] can suggest someone who meets these qualifications, we will be grateful to you. A stamped, addressed envelope is[7] enclosed for your convenience. Very truly yours, [149]

308 Dear Mr. Smith: Does your insurance program consist of many different policies? Do you have one policy[1] for theft, another policy for fire, and still another for liability? If you do, you are probably paying[2] more for your *protection** than you need to.

We have one policy, Mr. Smith, that is designed to include every[3] *kind*† of coverage a business can need. It simplifies your insurance problem because you deal with one[4] company and pay one premium.

The next time you are thinking of reviewing your insurance plans, call us. You[5] will find that we are able to provide just the protection you need and save you money in the bargain. Yours very[6] truly, [121] *Also correct:*
*insurance
†type

LESSON 37

313 Dear Mr. Thomas: All Nashville Insurance offices have one thing in common: They have very special agents.[1] Thousands of people look to these agents for advice on problems of financial security and protection.[2] Why do they choose Nashville agents? The reason is that they know Nashville agents are very special. They are carefully[3] chosen and well trained. They are the kind of men and women you like to do business with.

Furthermore, every[4] Nashville agent is part of a team. Supplementing his efforts are experts in every phase of life insurance.[5] Their experience is at his disposal in planning a life insurance program for you.

That is why so[6] many thousands of people have a Nashville agent advise them when they have financial problems, and that is why[7] a Nashville agent is a good man to know.

Call him today. Sincerely yours, [154]

314 Dear Mr. Baker: If your house were on fire, could you get out safely? Whether or not you could will depend on how[1] level-headed you are and how much planning ahead you have done.

You might think that you could just rush out of the front[2] door, but what if flames have trapped you upstairs? Would you know how to escape from there? What about the rest of the family?[3] Would you be able to evacuate them safely?

If you haven't considered these questions before, we advise[4] you to do so now.

To help people like you, the Omaha Insurance Company is offering a short, simple[5] guide on how to plan escape routes for your whole family. It is called *How to Get Out of a Burning Building.*[6] To obtain your copy, stop in at our office at any time that is convenient. If you prefer, fill out and[7] mail the enclosed card. When we receive it, we will mail you a copy. Very truly yours, [157]

315 Dear Mr. Day: Your letter of June 15 containing your check to cover your premium on policy No.[1] 112156 arrived yesterday, June 18. Unfortunately, it arrived ten days after your[2] grace period had expired, and we had to cancel your policy.

However, we can write you a new policy[3] that will provide the same coverages as your former policy at a premium of $50[4] a month, or only $4 a month more than you have been paying.

If this suggestion appeals to you, complete[5] the enclosed application form and return it to us together with your first month's premium of $50.[6] An envelope is enclosed for your convenience. Cordially yours, [133]

316 Dear Mr. Beane: Transactions involving merchandise and services in today's business world are based on credit.[1] Yet extending credit often involves some risk, too. Some companies have seen their full year's profits wiped out by credit[2] losses. That is why more and more businesses today carry credit insurance.

The North Dakota Insurance[3] Company pays you when your customers cannot. It protects you against their inability to pay as[4] a result of fire, bankruptcy, and other causes.

Return the enclosed postcard, and one of our agents will call[5] to give you full information about our plan that helps you prevent credit losses. Sincerely yours, [118]

317 Dear Mr. Casey: If one of

your trusted employees stole several hundred thousand dollars from you, could your[1] company survive? Unfortunately, employee dishonesty is the direct cause of many business failures.[2] It causes more failures than the result of fires, natural disasters, and legal action. Each year businessmen[3] lose billions of dollars to their own employees.

You can protect your business by taking out dishonesty[4] insurance. The cost of this type of insurance is surprisingly low. Would you like to know more about dishonesty[5] insurance? We will be glad to tell you all about it; simply sign and return the enclosed card. Very[6] truly yours,   [122]

318   Dear Mr. Burlington: The premium on your life insurance, which should have been paid on March 1, is now past due.[1] Although you are still covered, the 30-day grace period ends on Friday, March 30—just 10 days from now. We know[2] that the protection and welfare of your family are *matters** of great importance to you. We know, too, that you[3] would not *want*† to leave your loved ones unprotected by letting your policy lapse.

As your policy expires in[4] 10 days, it is imperative that you act immediately. Do not delay. If you want to continue your[5] current policy, send us a check for $28 today. An airmail reply envelope is enclosed[6] for your convenience. Sincerely yours,   [127]
Also correct:
*things
†wish

LESSON 38

322   Dear Mr. Nelson: We have come to realize that helping our customers understand their insurance is almost[1] as important as selling it to them.

Two years ago we at the Denison Insurance Company decided[2] to open an Office of Insurance Information. This office is run by well-trained people, who have[3] only one objective: Helping our clients understand their insurance.

Since this office was opened, we have had over[4] 40,000 inquiries concerning insurance problems. We found that many people were confused about[5] their insurance.

If you would like to know how your insurance works, how no-fault automobile insurance affects[6] you, or whether your present coverage is inadequate, call the Office of Insurance Information today.[7] We will do our best to answer your questions. Sincerely yours,   [152]

323   Dear Mr. Decker: Disabilities from sickness or accident happen every day. You may think that nothing[1] is going to happen to you, but you are no more immune than the next person. At any time you may be the[2] victim of some other person's carelessness.

If you have one of our accident insurance policies, you need[3] not worry about how you will pay your hospital and doctors' bills. You will be fully protected during any[4] period of illness or disability. If you should become totally disabled, your policy[5] automatically becomes paid up. In addition, we will send you a monthly check for the rest of your life.[6] The amount you will receive will depend, of course, on the type and amount of your policy.

Return the enclosed[7] form for full information; you will be placing yourself under no obligation. Very truly yours, [158]

324 Dear Mr. Douglas: Our sincere welcome to you as a new client of the New York Insurance Agency, one[1] of the largest, most respected agencies in the city. The services of our company are at your disposal.[2]

As you were informed by the R. B. Miller Agency, we are taking over their fire and casualty[3] insurance, which they are discontinuing on August 1.

The enclosed policy is the renewal of your[4] insurance policy No. 117716. It is submitted for your approval. If you have had[5] your property appraised recently and the value shown on the policy is inconsistent with the appraisal,[6] you may wish to change the amount of your insurance. If that is the case, please let us know; we will be glad to[7] make any adjustments you suggest.

Whenever we can be of help in serving your insurance needs, please feel free[8] to call on us. Yours very truly, [167]

325 Gentlemen: Next month I plan to buy a new car, and I would like to purchase automobile insurance from your[1] company. I understand that no-fault insurance is now in force in our state and that this should mean a reduction[2] in premiums.

I do not, however, understand all the aspects of the new insurance regulations.[3] I would appreciate it, therefore, if one of your representatives would call on me to discuss the matter.[4]

It would be most convenient for me if someone could come to my home after 6 o'clock any evening next[5] week. Sincerely yours, [103]

326 Dear Mr. Jackson: In recent years business failures have reached new highs. Suppose a customer's business fails. Will you[1] be able to collect any money that he owes you? You won't have to worry about this if you have protected[2] yourself with American bad-debt insurance. When you carry this insurance, you will be paid if a customer[3] goes bankrupt.

To learn more about American bad-debt insurance, simply fill out and mail the[4] enclosed card. Very sincerely yours, [87]

327 Dear Mr. Young: Do you realize that 40 percent of all businesses that suffer damage by fire, floods, or[1] windstorms never reopen? It is true that they *carry*° insurance on their buildings, their furniture, and their stock.[2] However, they do not carry insurance that provides them with income while repairs are being made. Consequently,[3] they are incapable of carrying on their regular business operations during the period[4] of reconstruction and are forced out of business.

A *simple*† answer to this problem is to buy income protection⁵ insurance. This type of insurance provides businesses with income that helps them survive a period when⁶ their plant is closed because of fire or some other catastrophe.

May we tell you more about this valuable⁷ insurance, Mr. Young? A letter or a telephone call will bring one of our men to your office to give you⁸ complete details. Very truly yours, [167]

Also correct:
*have, own
†easy, effective

LESSON 39

330 Dear Mr. Morgan: Can you receive a regular income from your life insurance during your lifetime? If you¹ have a permanent life insurance policy, the answer is yes.

This type of policy gives you several² options, and one of them permits you to exchange your life policy for a lifetime income.

Naturally, the³ amount of the payments you receive will depend on the amount you have invested in your policy.

If you⁴ would like to know more about permanent life insurance, sign and return the enclosed card. When we receive it, we⁵ will send you a copy of our fact-filled 45-page booklet, *Benefits of Life Insurance.* Sincerely yours,⁶ [120]

331 Dear Mr. Hanson: Your letter suggesting that one should have his property appraised frequently for fire insurance¹ purposes made me realize that my home may not be adequately protected.

I would appreciate² it, therefore, if you would ask one of your representatives to appraise my property.

Please call me at³ 116-1185 for an appointment. Sincerely yours, [70]

332 To the Staff: On Friday, April 15, our management committee established a policy that we maintain¹ a file on the car insurance carried by all members of the staff who use their personal cars on company² business. This policy applies to all employees, whether they use their cars every day or only once or³ twice a year.

A form is attached for your convenience in supplying this information. Please fill it out and return⁴ it to Miss Janice Green, head of our accounting department, on or before May 1. M. L. Baker [98]

333 To the Staff: The suggestion has been made by our insurance company that we make available to our¹ employees a course in defensive driving. We have decided to require such a course for all employees who drive² on company business.

In the future, any employee who wishes to be reimbursed for car expenses³ must have completed this course.

The course will be conducted by members of the local police force in Room 28⁴ of our main building. It will consist of four 2-hour sessions on Mondays and Wednesdays beginning on June 4[5] at 3 p.m. It is completely described in the enclosed bulletin.

Please arrange to enroll in the program[6] either through your district manager or through the personnel department. A. C. James [135]

334 Dear Mr. Wright: Thank you for placing your insurance with the American Mutual Insurance Company.[1] You have become a policyholder in one of the most distinguished insurance companies in the world.[2]

American Mutual supplies insurance for people in all walks of life. Through our 4,000 representatives[3] we serve millions of people ranging from small shopkeepers to the presidents of giant organizations.[4] Our size and versatility enable us to serve the smallest as well as the largest accounts. Yet we give[5] personal attention to every account.

If there is any other information you would like to have[6] concerning the features of your new insurance policy, please call us.

Welcome, Mr. Wright, to our family[7] of policyholders. Sincerely yours, [147]

335 Dear Mr. Davis: Why should the car insurance premiums you pay cover accidents caused by careless drivers?[1] We do not think this is fair, and we have decided to do something about it. We have devised an insurance[2] plan° that enables the careful driver to pay a smaller premium than the careless driver.

Our preferred risk[3] insurance plan, which is offered to careful drivers only, enables you to purchase automobile insurance[4] at rates that are probably much lower than those that you are now paying.

You owe it to yourself, Mr. Davis,[5] to *obtain*† the facts about our special rates and to compare them with those that you are now paying. You may be[6] able to save yourself a considerable sum on your next policy. Sincerely yours, [137]

Also correct:

°policy, program

†get, learn

LESSON 40

338 *Planning Insurance*

Everyone, single or married, should realize that his death will result in expenses someone will have to[1] pay. He should also realize that the end of his useful income-earning years, through disability or[2] retirement, can create another financial burden. Besides death expenses and retirement needs, other insurable[3] requirements apply to those who have financial dependents.

A sensible way to plan a life insurance[4] program is to list the most common financial needs that would arise after the loss of a family[5] breadwinner.

Insurance planning should start with a clean-up fund to meet all the expenses that arise immediately[6] after death. Consider the following, for example:

How will the family pay the first monthly bills, the[7] charge accounts, and the installment payments? These expenses, together with the funeral and last-illness costs,[8] necessitate a clean-up fund.

Then a readjustment fund is necessary for the family to adjust to[9] its new way of living. Decisions must be made—whether the members of the family can stay together and[10] whether they can keep the home—that are better done under the quiet, unhurried conditions that a carefully[11] planned insurance program gives the survivors.

Now if the family man wants to help his family continue[12] as a unit until the children are old enough to take on the responsibilities of their own upkeeping,[13] he must plan his insurance even further ahead so that there will be a family income during the[14] children's maturing years.

The ideal insurance program provides for two more contingencies: (1) an education[15] fund for the children and (2) a retirement income fund.

This type of program—for complete coverage, including[16] retirement—is highly desirable. However, it should be remembered that the primary purpose[17] of life insurance is to protect the family if the breadwinner dies. [354]—Adapted from *Insurance for Credit Unions*

339 *Ordinary Life Insurance*

Ordinary life insurance can be used to meet almost every conceivable type of personal or[1] business need in which protection of human values and loss of earning power are at stake. It is the oldest[2] of the three classifications of life insurance.

Ordinary life insurance is used to provide not only[3] a sum of money to enable one to "die even with the world" but also a continuing income to[4] a widow and children, making it possible to keep the home together. In addition, it is purchased to[5] provide a life income to the widow after the children are grown. It can pay the children's way through college and retire[6] the mortgage on the family home.

People use ordinary life insurance not only for protection[7] but also as a means of accumulating money for their own use later in life when they have outlived[8] the need for insurance protection. The value of the policy may then be taken either in one sum or[9] in an income that will continue as long as the insured lives.

In addition to these individual and[10] family uses, ordinary life insurance is frequently used in the business world to insure the lives[11] of business executives and other key men for the benefit of the business. In small corporations and[12] partnerships, part owners are often insured. This makes it possible, when a part owner dies, to pay his family[13] promptly a prearranged price for his interest in the business. It enables the surviving part owners[14] to continue the business. It avoids delay in settlement or even liquidation.

As you can see,[15] ordinary life insurance has quite a number of worthwhile uses.

Premiums for ordinary policies[16] are usually paid directly to the company annually, semiannually, quarterly, or[17] sometimes even monthly. Policies are almost always issued in units of $1,000 or more. A[18] medical examination is frequently required of each applicant for a policy. [377]

How Big Should My Shorthand Be?

Each writer must set his own size for his shorthand writing. Whatever size seems right to you is probably the best[1] size for you. One skillful shorthand reporter writes 500 words of shorthand on an ordinary notebook page;[2] another writes only 50 words on a similar page. Neither extreme is recommended. If you naturally[3] find yourself writing very large notes or very small notes, you need not be concerned about the size of your notes.[4]

If you write whatever size of shorthand notes seems to be natural for you, the size will have little or no effect[5] on your speed. If you try constantly to write notes larger or smaller than you would naturally write, you may[6] find that the attempt to change the size of your notes hinders the development of your speed. [132] —*Martin J. Dupraw*

Chapter 9

LESSON 41

342 Gentlemen: To remain healthy, our present economy requires greater production in all manufacturing[1] industries. In order to obtain this greater production, many big, successful companies are considering[2] the important advantages of building plants in the Atlanta area. These advantages include[3] the following:

1. Room for expansion
2. An ample labor supply
3. Satisfactory living[4] conditions
4. A good climate

If you would like to have a circular describing these advantages as they apply[5] to your particular business, let us know; we will send it to you promptly.

We hope that one day we may have[6] the opportunity to welcome your organization to the Atlanta area. Sincerely yours,[7] [140]

343 Dear Mr. Smith: Would you like to increase your profits from the sale of your products to the Common Market? Then build[1] a plant in Ireland.

Ireland is the gateway to Europe. With our modern transportation facilities, shipping[2] to any Common Market city is fast, easy, and economical. What is more, Ireland offers you these[3] attractive incentives:

1. No taxes on all export profits for 15 years.
2. A large, well-trained labor force to[4] operate your plant profitably.
3. Financial aid to help you build your plant.

We will be glad to give you complete[5] information about the advantages Ireland offers businessmen if you will fill out and return the enclosed[6] card. Sincerely yours, [123]

344 Mr. Ryan: On Friday, July 15, we received a large order for our flooring materials from the Baker[1] Company of Albany.

As you know, we have been striving for many years without success to win this account.[2] Now that we have won them over, let us do our best to keep them happy.

When you are in the vicinity of[3] Albany, I suggest that you stop in to see Mr. Baker and the other officers of the company.[4] It will be a nice gesture of goodwill. R. L. Wilson [90]

345 Gentlemen: If you are looking for an ideal location to build a new manufacturing plant, we invite[1] you to inspect the facilities of the Jackson Industrial Park.

Located just south of the city, the[2] Jackson Industrial Park provides a perfect place for light manufacturing industries.

The park is near a[3] railroad, a major highway, and the Jackson airport. In addition, the Jackson area has an adequate[4] labor supply. The fine technical schools in this area provide an excellent work force.

Before you decide[5] on a site on which to build your next plant, come to see us. You will be glad you did. Sincerely yours, [117]

346 Dear Mr. Hastings: During the past two or three months we have been receiving complaints from the citizens of Springfield[1] who live in the neighborhood of your manufacturing plant to the effect that the air pollution is[2] becoming worse.

After discussing the matter of pollution with you last March, I am convinced that your organization[3] is making progress in installing equipment that will help control the quality of the air in the[4] neighborhood. In view of the complaints we have received, however, I feel it would be wise for you to make a public[5] statement to the people informing them of the steps you have taken and are taking to improve the quality[6] of the air.

If you would like to discuss the matter with me further, please do not hesitate to call me. Sincerely[7] yours, [141]

347 Dear Mr. Paine: As you know, we have recently opened a plant in Memphis to manufacture ladies' clothing.[1] We feel that it would benefit us to become a member of the Memphis Chamber of Commerce.

While we have only[2] recently *begun** to do business in the South, we have been manufacturing ladies' clothing for over[3] 25 years in other parts of the country. We request, therefore, that we be given the opportunity[4] to become a member of the Memphis Chamber of Commerce.

If you will send us the necessary application[5] forms, we will be grateful. Sincerely yours, [109]
Also correct:
*started

LESSON 42

352 Dear Mr. Smith: The shipment of four tables that we ordered from you on June 27 was delivered on Friday[1] morning, July 5. When one of our men opened the crates on July 6, he found that all four tables had been[2] so badly damaged that we cannot accept them.

Please arrange to have one of your trucks pick up the damaged tables[3] as soon as possible and send us four new ones.

We hope to hear from you soon. Yours very truly,   [77]

353   Dear Mr. Davis: We were distressed to learn that the tables you ordered arrived at your warehouse in poor condition.[1] Our shipping department is looking into the matter to determine whether the damage was the result[2] of improper packing or of carelessness on the trucking company's part.

A new shipment is on its way to[3] you to replace the damaged tables. Mr. Clark, our representative in your area, will come to see you[4] within the next few days. He will arrange to have the damaged tables returned to us.

We are sorry for the[5] inconvenience you have been caused, Mr. Davis, and assure you that we will make every effort to see that future[6] shipments arrive in first-class condition. Sincerely yours,   [131]

354   Mr. Day: On Friday, July 8, we received a letter from the Bennington Company of Cincinnati[1] indicating that they had received a shipment from us in very poor condition. This merchandise was delivered[2] to Cincinnati by the Western Trucking Company.

Please discuss this matter immediately with the[3] packer who had charge of crating this merchandise. I would like to know whether the damage was the result of[4] negligence on our part or of carelessness on the part of the trucking company. If the trucking company is[5] responsible, we will, of course, file a claim to recover the cost of the damage.

I have sent a memorandum[6] to the order department asking them to ship to the Bennington Company a replacement for the damaged[7] tables. R. J. Smith   [144]

355   Dear Mr. Cunningham: Our president, Mr. C. R. Smith, passed on to me your request for credit information[1] about the Princeton Manufacturing Company.

We have done a great deal of business with the Princeton[2] Manufacturing Company during the past three years, and during that time we have never had to send them so much[3] as a reminder that their account was past due. In fact, on all but two occasions they have taken advantage[4] of the 2 percent discount that we allow for payment of bills within ten days of our billing date.

If you should[5] grant credit to the Princeton Manufacturing Company, we are sure you will be pleased with their efficient, cooperative[6] method of doing business. If you would like to have further information, be sure to let us know;[7] we will be glad to supply it. Very truly yours,   [150]

356   Dear Mr. Green: On July 2 we sent you our order No. 2543 for a carload of lumber. As[1] we have had a fire in our warehouse in Orlando where we had planned to store this lumber, we are forced to cancel[2] this order.

We hope that we will have the warehouse rebuilt within a month or so. As soon as we do, we will reorder[3] the lumber. Very truly yours, [67]

357 Gentlemen: Because our business has been expanding so rapidly, we are planning to build a new plant to[1] manufacture automobile parts. We are considering three or four sites for this plant, and one of them is Newark.[2]

Do you have any material you can *send** us about available sites in the Newark area? Any[3] site we *select†* will have to be near a major highway, a railroad depot, and an airport.

We would also[4] like to have any information you can give us about the availability of skilled and unskilled labor[5] in the area. Cordially yours, [107]
Also correct:
*mail, give
†choose, decide on

LESSON 43

361 Dear Mr. Green: The Kentucky Advertising Council has invited me to speak at one of the general[1] sessions of its biannual conference, which will be held in Louisville on July 1, 2, and 3. At this[2] session I plan to speak on the basic principles that paper manufacturers follow in advertising[3] their various products.

As almost everyone is aware, the amount of paper used in food packaging[4] has increased considerably during the past few years, and indications are that the demand for food packaging[5] paper will continue to increase in the years ahead. Since your organization is one of the largest,[6] best-known producers of paper for the food industry, it occurred to me that you might be willing to tell me[7] about the basic principles your company follows in advertising its paper.

I am sure that in the[8] preparation of my talk I could advantageously use any information you supply me.

If you have[9] any printed literature on the subject, I would appreciate receiving that as well. Sincerely yours,[10] [200]

362 Dear Mr. Winters: It is indeed a pleasure to send you the enclosed copy of the guidelines we have developed[1] for advertising our paper products. In developing these guidelines, we have had the cooperation[2] of Wilson Associates, a local advertising agency.

As you may know, the paper industry is[3] giving serious attention to reducing the pollution of our waterways. Since you may be interested[4] in devoting a portion of your talk to this topic, we are also enclosing a copy of a pamphlet[5] entitled *The Paper Industry and Ecology.*

If we can be of further help, please get in touch with[6] us. Sincerely yours, [123]

363 Dear Mr. Green: Thank you very much for your letter and the material you sent me. I was particularly[1] pleased to learn of your independent efforts to improve the environment of our country.

In the pamphlet,[2] reference is

made to a film, *Improving our Water,* that your company has produced describing specific[3] steps it is taking to find the solution of the problem of pollution control. If the film is available,[4] I would like very much to show it to the students of our local high school. Will you please send me further[5] information about this film. Cordially yours, [109]

364 Gentlemen: In July I will be moving to Houston, and I would like to apply for a position with your[1] paper manufacturing company. A complete personal data sheet is enclosed.

For the past five years I[2] have worked for the Central Paper Company in Jacksonville. I find it necessary for personal reasons[3] to move to Houston. The manager of the Central Paper Company, Mr. E. H. Mason, has graciously[4] given me permission to use his name as a reference.

If you have an opening and are interested[5] in considering my application, please let me know. I will be happy to come for an interview at your[6] convenience. Yours very truly, [124]

365 Gentlemen: On June 2 I purchased from your store a Johnson toaster. When the toaster arrived, it was not the model[1] I ordered; therefore, I returned it to you immediately for credit.

When I received my July statement,[2] I found that you had not given me credit for $18, the cost of the toaster.

Will you please correct[3] your records so that this charge will not appear on my August statement. Yours very truly, [76]

366 Dear Mr. Green: We are sorry that we still cannot ship the five adding machines you ordered on April 10.

This[1] delay is caused by the fact that we have not been able to get a number of the parts we need.

We are told that[2] the parts will be in our factory in a few days. As soon as the adding machines are ready, we will have them[3] delivered to you by our own truck. Yours very truly, [70]

367 Dear Mr. Sanford: On Friday, April 16, we received a letter from the Wilson Company requesting[1] us to open an account for them. They told us that for three years they have been purchasing merchandise from you on[2] open account and that you would be able to supply us with credit information.

We would appreciate it,[3] Mr. Sanford, if you would complete the enclosed form and *return** it to us. We would also like to have any[4] further information that will help us determine how much credit we should grant the Wilson Company.

All[5] information you furnish us will, of course, be held in strict confidence.

A stamped, addressed envelope is enclosed for[6] your convenience. Yours very truly, [125]
Also correct:
*mail, send

LESSON 44

371 Dear Mr. Starr: For the past two years I have been comparing the many types of automobile tires on the market[1] to determine the ones that are the best buys. I have summarized the information I have acquired in an[2] article entitled "Economy in Buying Tires." This article should be of interest to your subscribers;[3] therefore, I am submitting it to you for publication in your magazine, *Consumer's Digest.*

I am[4] sending the manuscript to you separately; it should reach you in a day or so. I hope you will give my article[5] favorable consideration. Sincerely yours, [110]

372 Dear Mr. Bates: Thank you for sending us your article, "Economy in Buying Tires," for possible publication.[1] It has been critically read by two members of our editorial staff, both of whom feel that it contains[2] much practical information.

Unfortunately, the manuscripts we have already accepted for publication[3] are sufficient to provide us with material for the rest of the year. Under the circumstances,[4] we have decided not to purchase additional manuscripts until next December. By that time we feel the[5] information in your report will be too dated to be of value.

Thank you very much, Mr. Bates, for thinking[6] of *Consumer's Digest.* When you prepare other articles in the future that you think will be of interest[7] to our subscribers, we will be happy to review them. Sincerely yours, [153]

373 Gentlemen: The annual fall fashion show will be held in the New York Coliseum on March 1, 2, and 3. We[1] presume that your company will again wish to exhibit at this show.

We have not yet received your application[2] for exhibit space, and we are concerned that you might miss the deadline for registration.

To date, we have over[3] 100 clothing manufacturers who have accepted invitations to exhibit their new lines. We[4] expect the final number to be well over 200.

Buyers from every state in the country will be here[5] to make selections for the coming season.

Don't miss this opportunity to show your new line of clothing. Fill[6] out the application blank that is enclosed and return it in the postage-paid envelope with your check for[7] $100. Sincerely yours, [146]

374 Dear Mr. West: Enclosed is our completed application and a check for $100 to cover the[1] registration fee to exhibit our new line at the fall fashion show in New York in March.

Frankly, we had let[2] the date "slip up" on us. Thanks for reminding us that we needed to get the application in before the deadline.[3]

We have exhibited our clothing at the show for the past seven years, and we certainly had no intention[4] of missing this year's show. We consider this show an essential part of our marketing plans.

We look forward[5] to presenting our fall line in New York. Cordially yours, [110]

375 Dear Mr. Roberts: Your idea for conducting a safety campaign in your factory is an excellent[1] one, and our company will be glad to work with you on the program. We can supply various types of visual[2] aids to draw attention to safety on the job. Our experience has been that the greatest difficulty[3] is selling the idea of safety to the workers. Once you have their cooperation, the battle is[4] half won.

One way to sell safety is through a series of colorful, well-planned safety posters that depict potentially[5] dangerous situations in a humorous way.

If it will be convenient, one of our representatives[6] will visit your factory on February 3 to discuss the ways in which we can help you in your[7] campaign. Sincerely yours, [143]

376 Gentlemen: On Friday, June 15, we gave your salesman, Mr. Charles Brown, our order No. 1181 for[1] five garden chairs. Mr. Brown promised us that these chairs would be delivered by July 5. Today is July 6,[2] but the chairs have not yet arrived. If we do not receive them immediately, they will not be available[3] for our annual summer sale.

May we expect to receive these garden chairs within the next few days? If not, we[4] will have no alternative but to cancel our order. Yours truly, [93]

377 Dear Mr. Green: It is my pleasant duty, as chairman of the Community Chest drive at the Wilson Manufacturing[1] Company, to tell you that all our employees have pledged to make a contribution to this year's campaign.[2] On Friday, June 15, we received the last of the pledges from our Washington Street branch.

I hope, Mr. Green,[3] that other *companies** in the city will be as successful in obtaining pledges from their employees as[4] we have been. If they are, the city should be able to exceed substantially the goal of $10,000,000.[5]

I am preparing a final report on my activities as chairman, and I will send you a copy as[6] soon as it is ready. Sincerely yours, [127]
Also correct:
*organizations

LESSON 45

380 *History of the Capitol Building*

Our nation's Capitol looks out over Washington, with its wings widespread and its white dome thrust toward the sun, like the[1] American eagle itself. The resolutions of the Congress that sits there influence the destiny of[2] 200,000,000 Americans and the councils of every foreign office on earth.

From its conception,[3] the Capitol was as dear to George Washington as if it were the Constitution in stone. He himself laid the[4] cornerstone on September 18, 1793, while cannons boomed a salute to the future.

Designs[5] for the home of Congress had been invited by a contest in which the prize was the grand sum of $500,[6] plus a lot in the unbuilt city. The specifications were for a building containing two lofty chambers[7] for Senate and House, each capable of holding 300 persons (including spectators), with two lobbies[8] and twelve offices for committees and clerks.

Washington and Jefferson, who were the judges of the contest, inclined[9] at first toward the plans of a Paris-trained architect, Stephen Hallet. A novice architect named William Thornton[10] of Philadelphia entered the contest and won the grand prize. Hallet was later hired to supervise the[11] building of the Capitol but was promptly dismissed when it was found he was substituting some of his original[12] building designs.

The Capitol reached completion only after endless alterations. Congress, like many[13] home builders, was swamped by unforeseen costs. Contractors cheated Uncle Sam—the shingle roof leaked, wall plaster crumbled,[14] and a chandelier fell out of the ceiling. The acoustics were so faulty that the precious "pearls of oratory"[15] often floated to the roof and were lost.

Yet by 1812 the Capitol was, for all of its defects,[16] complete in the modest dignity that befitted the era. Fine portraits of our early heroes adorned its[17] walls. It housed a wealth of precious documents as well as the Congressional Library.

Then war with Great Britain[18] broke out. In August of 1814, by a surprise dash up the Potomac, the British fleet captured the defenseless[19] city and set the noble building afire.

When peace came, the walls alone remained intact. Benjamin Latrobe,[20] whose talents were noted by President Jefferson, was placed in charge of its reconstruction. He was responsible[21] for many of the beautiful details in the building—notably the use of American motifs[22] like ears of corn and tobacco leaves atop the columns instead of the previous Greek detail.

Not long after[23] its home was rebuilt, Congress realized that it had outgrown the building. What had started out as a small group of[24] 13 states along the Atlantic seaboard had, by 1851, spread across the continent. Both[25] chambers were packed as the forces of the South, the expanding West, and the East were locked in tense struggles. Hundreds of[26] clerks jostled one another for space. Members from the new states were demanding offices. The Library was bursting[27] at the seams, and books were spreading down the halls. The Supreme Court, which at first had very few cases to consider,[28] was now busy and elbowing for room.

So were begun the two great wings, in one of which the Senators established[29] themselves and in the other the Representatives.   [590]

381 Gentlemen: On July 18 your truck delivered to us the desk we purchased from your store on July 10. When[1] we opened the crate in which the desk was shipped, we found that one of the legs was broken.

Please have your truck pick up this[2] desk as soon as possible. Yours truly,   [47]

Chapter 10

LESSON 46

384 Dear Mr. Cross: How much mail can your postage meter handle? From morning to afternoon the typewriters in your[1] office work away, with most of their output ending up as mail. Then, usually between 4 and 5 o'clock,[2] this mail descends on the mailroom to pass through your postage meter one piece at a time, causing a jam in the mailroom.[3]

If your present meter must face an ever-increasing amount of mail, the solution is a Crane postage[4] meter. It can take a pile of letters or circulars of almost any size and weight and automatically[5] print the correct postage on each piece.

For more information about the Crane postage meter, return the enclosed[6] card. Yours very truly, [124]

385 Dear Mr. Layton: You will always make a good impression when you use Smith stencils and inks in preparing office[1] bulletins, forms, and reports. These stencils and inks make an unbeatable team.

Each duplicating job "comes alive"[2] when it is run on a Smith stencil. The sensitive plastic coat of the stencil makes copy after copy[3] so uniformly clear that they resemble top-quality printing. Experience has shown, too, that Smith stencils[4] give much longer runs than ordinary ones.

Smith duplicator inks yield the maximum number of clear, sharp copies[5] from each stencil without becoming gummy. They are available in a wide variety of colors.[6]

If you would like complete inforation about Smith quality office supplies, return the enclosed card. Yours very[7] truly, [141]

386 Dear Mr. Martin: In many business organizations, sending out a big mailing creates difficult problems.[1] Highly paid workers are diverted from their regular jobs to fold and stuff circulars and other advertising[2] material into envelopes in order to meet a mailing deadline. The operation of the office[3] is disrupted, and important work must be neglected.

This will not happen, however, in an organization[4] that has installed a Harper Mailer 161. This unit folds mailing pieces, inserts them in envelopes,[5] and seals the envelopes at the rate of 5,000 an hour. Thus in one ordinary working day you can[6] process as many as 40,000 pieces while your regular staff goes about its regular duties.

Wouldn't[7] you like to have us install a Harper 161 in your office on a ten-day trial basis? To arrange[8] this, simply return the enclosed card. Very truly yours, [171]

387 Dear Mr. Mead: We are pleased to announce the new Wilson comprehensive office machine repair service. For only[1] $200 we will keep your duplicators and calculators in perfect operating condition[2] for an entire year. We are sure that you will want to take advantage of this opportunity to free yourself[3] of all service worries concerning your equipment.

This plan includes an initial visit by our serviceman[4] to clean your machines and make necessary repairs. Then during the year, if your machines should need service, you[5] simply telephone us; one of our servicemen will come to your office promptly. If he cannot repair the machine[6] in your office, he will leave a replacement while he takes your machine to our shop for repair.

Why not call us[7] today and subscribe to our comprehensive office machine repair service. Cordially yours, [155]

388 Dear Mr. Casey: Would you like to be relieved of the headaches of running a bookkeeping department? Then let[1] the National Data Processing Company take over your company's bookkeeping. If you will return the[2] enclosed card, we will send you our booklet that describes our services. Here is what we will do for you:

1. Save you[3] money and overhead
2. Prepare your local, state, and federal tax reports
3. Take care of your accounts receivable and[4] accounts payable
4. Prepare your payroll

You need not buy or rent any expensive equipment; we have our[5] own. You will never be asked to sign a contract. If you are not satisfied with our service, you can terminate our[6] services at any time.

These are a few of the reasons why more than 15,000 firms use our services. We[7] would like to add your firm to our list of customers, Mr. Casey. Cordially yours, [154]

389 Dear Mr. James: When customers call and ask you questions about shipping dates, back orders, and other matters[1] pertaining to orders, can you give them accurate information while they are still on the phone? If you cannot, you[2] need a more dependable order processing system.

You will be able to get* the information your customers[3] need in seconds if you have a Johnson microfilm system. This system puts all your vital order records[4] into a simple film file and makes them available for instant reference.

Are you interested? If[5] you are, fill out and mail the enclosed form. When we receive it, we will send† you a free portfolio describing[6] the advantages of a Johnson microfilm system. Sincerely yours, [133]
Also correct:
*obtain, gather
†mail

LESSON 47

394 Dear Mr. Stans: Several days ago the Office Management Association of Danville decided to[1] hold its annual exhibit of business machines on Friday, March 16, in the National Hotel.

We are[2] sure that you will be glad to have an opportunity once again to see the finest office equipment[3] manufactured today.

The Brown Office Equipment Company will, of course, be represented. We have been assigned[4] Booth 15. In addition to our regular line of machines, we will have on display our Model 1818[5] electronic calculator, the newest, smallest, and least expensive calculator on the market. We[6] know that you will want to see this unique calculator as well as the other machines we will have on display.[7]

Enclosed are two tickets to the exhibit; we hope you will be able to use them. Cordially yours,   [158]

395 Dear Mr. Tyler: We understand that you are planning to install a learning laboratory at Knoxville[1] Community College. We would like to show you the Rushmore listening laboratory equipment. The Rushmore is[2] the newest and finest listening laboratory available today. It can be used in both business and language[3] classes and may be used for group as well as individual instruction.

The Rushmore is designed to[4] enable your students to choose from eight broadcast channels simply by dialing the correct station on their headsets.

May[5] we have the opportunity to demonstrate the Rushmore to you? Just indicate on the enclosed card a time[6] that will be convenient for you. I will then arrange to have a well-trained representative visit you. Sincerely[7] yours,   [141]

396 Dear Mr. Layton: Yes, we are planning to install several learning laboratories at Knoxville Community[1] College. We plan to equip our laboratories with cassette players rather than reel-to-reel equipment, and[2] the Rushmore model may be the type that will fit our needs.

I might add, however, that we plan to operate almost[3] entirely on an individual-instruction basis, and we

need equipment that is flexible. We[4] plan to equip at least three laboratories for use in a variety of ways, enabling the individual[5] student to operate the equipment and to progress at his own rate.

We would appreciate it[6] if your company's representative would call on us and demonstrate the Rushmore. Yours very truly,   [138]

397 Dear Mr. Fisher: We were glad to receive your letter telling us of your intention to replace 20 of[1] your present tape recorders with standard cassette tape players. We are convinced that the cassette tape player is the[2] most flexible playback unit now available for individual instruction.

We are enclosing a[3] brochure that describes our newest model, the Howard 1211. This attractive lightweight machine has a rubber[4] base that keeps it from slipping off the desk. The magnetic heads provide fine playback clarity, and earphones are[5] available on an optional basis.

When I received your letter, I called our dealer in Jacksonville and[6] suggested to him that he call you for an appointment to see you and tell you all about the Howard 1211[7] cassette tape player. I am sure you will hear from him soon. Sincerely yours,   [154]

398 Dear Mr. Smith: Enclosed is our application for exhibit space at the St. Louis Business Equipment Exposition[1] to be held on April 10, 11 and 12.

We are sending in our application early this year[2] to be sure that we obtain a good location. Last year we were placed in the south corner of the exhibit hall,[3] and the number of people who visited our booth was disappointing.

Please send us as soon as possible a[4] copy of the floor layout indicating the space that will be assigned to us. Sincerely yours, [97]

399 Dear Mr. James: A picture is worth a thousand words! You will be convinced of this, Mr. James, when you look at the[1] beautiful picture of the new Simplex accounting machine on the enclosed folder. It will show you better than[2] we can tell you how small, compact, and well designed this new *machine**[*] is. But the picture cannot tell you how efficiently[3] it operates.

As everyone will agree, a demonstration is worth a thousand pictures. Why not[4] let one of our representatives bring a new Simplex to your office for a free demonstration.

You will be[5] surprised to learn how a machine that is so easy to operate can handle almost any *type*[†] of accounting[6] job.

If you would like to have a demonstration of the Simplex, indicate on the enclosed card the time that[7] will be most convenient for our representative to call. Cordially yours, [154]

Also correct:
**°model*
†kind

LESSON 48

403 Dear Doctor Banks: The Jennings Office Supply Company will have a grand opening on Monday, April 3, at[1] 1502 Main Street. At this central location we hope to be able to serve the needs of both business and[2] education.

We would like to extend a cordial invitation to you and your staff at Brookdale Business College[3] to attend an open house on Monday evening, March 27, from 7 to 9 o'clock.

At that[4] time we will have on display the latest office furniture, equipment, and supplies.

We hope, Doctor Banks, that you[5] and your staff will be able to attend. Sincerely yours, [110]

404 Dear Mr. Thomas: Thank you for your letter inviting the staff of Brookdale Business College to attend a[1] special open house on Monday, March 27.

Unfortunately, we have an open house of our own that[2] evening for friends of our school. Our entire staff will be involved; consequently, none of us will be able to[3] attend your open house.

At the present time we are preparing to furnish a new library, and we are[4] interested in purchasing new desks and chairs for the room.

Although our school in Brookdale is 60 miles from Hartford,[5] we hope that you will ask one of your representatives to call on us to tell us about your line of desks and[6] chairs. Yours very truly, [124]

405 Dear Doctor Banks: We are indeed sorry that you and your staff will be unable to attend our open house on[1] the 27th of March.

Mr. A. R. Black, one of our sales

representatives, will be in Brookdale early[2] in April. He will call you for an appointment when he arrives to discuss with you our complete line of desks and[3] chairs.

In the meantime, perhaps you would like to look over the enclosed 16-page booklet that describes the various[4] types of desks and chairs that we have designed.

If you would like more information about our products prior to[5] Mr. Black's visit, please call us. We look forward to serving you. Sincerely yours, [114]

406 Dear Mr. Anderson: Have you seen our new $10,000 typewriter? If you have, you are not concerned with[1] its price.

If you have not, you will probably think we misplaced the decimal point in the figure. But the price is right![2] And so is the typewriter!

Our new General magnetic tape typewriter is well worth its cost. It is designed[3] to save your secretary's valuable time and your money because it never makes a mistake.

Here is how[4] the typewriter works. Your secretary types a dummy letter. When she strikes the wrong key, she simply backspaces[5] and strikes the correct key. Because the impression is being recorded on magnetic tape, the error simply[6] disappears after the strikeover.

When the dummy is finished, your secretary checks it, inserts a sheet of[7] letterhead, and presses a switch. Your letter is then typed error-free automatically.

Come in and let us[8] show you how an investment of $10,000 can save you many times that amount on the cost of your written[9] communications. Cordially yours, [187]

407 Dear Mr. James: A successful chemical company had a fire on its floor in a fireproof building. The fire[1] was not very severe, but the heat it generated ruined many irreplaceable records. The company[2] never again opened its doors.

Fire strikes a business every four minutes every day of the year,[3] and 93 percent of the victims are seriously handicapped because their records are destroyed.

The sure,[4] economical way to protect your records is to transfer them to Johnson files. These heavily insulated[5] files have saved irreplaceable records in hundreds of fires.

Take the first step to protect your records. Return[6] the enclosed card. When we receive it, we will send you our catalog of fireproof files and their prices. Cordially[7] yours, [141]

408 Dear Mr. Harding: Thank you for demonstrating for us the new General magnetic tape typewriter. After[1] you completed your demonstration, I recommended to the president that we purchase one of these machines.[2] However, I have just received the disappointing *news** that it will be necessary for us to defer the[3] purchase of all new equipment until January because of budgetary considerations.

As we[4] would like to begin using this equipment immediately, we would like to know if there is a *possibility*† that[5] we might rent the machine on a monthly basis. If there

is, please let me know the rental fee. Also, please let me[6] know whether the rental fee would be applied to the purchase price should we eventually decide to buy the[7] machine. Sincerely yours, [143]
Also correct:
°information
†chance

LESSON 49

412 Dear Mr. Dean: We have just placed on the market the Superior 3140 copier, the first compact[1] copier ever produced to sell for less than $200. Not only is it economical to[2] operate but it has also been simplified so as not to give mechanical troubles. And it takes up only[3] a little more space than an electric typewriter.

Because of all these outstanding features, the Superior[4] 3140 meets the copying needs of many people. For example, larger businesses will find the[5] Superior 3140 an ideal personal copier for supervisors and executives.[6] No longer will your personnel have to leave their desks to wait in line for copies.

To arrange for a demonstration[7] or to obtain more information about the Superior 3140, call 392-6140.[8] We will try to prove to you that a copier does not have to be expensive to be good. Sincerely yours,[9] [180]

413 Dear Miss Adams: If you are like most secretaries, you do not enjoy cleaning the keys of your typewriter before[1] you type a stencil. Cleaning keys will be no problem,

however, if you have a Benson type cleaner.

When you[2] use a Benson type cleaner, you do no more than strike the keys to clean your type. The Benson cleaner is a special[3] paper that rolls into your typewriter the same way an ordinary piece of paper does. You simply insert[4] the paper, set the machine for "stencil," and strike each key several times. The whole procedure takes only a few[5] seconds, and it leaves both you and your typewriter keys clean. No wonder it has won the approval of so many[6] secretaries who have tried it!

For a free sample, write to our distribution office at the address shown on[7] this letterhead. Make type cleaning a pleasure for a change! Sincerely yours, [153]

414 Dear Mr. Young: Jennings Enterprises cordially invites you to visit our new Office Systems Center at[1] 1776 West 42 Street. This center is not merely a showroom to promote office equipment;[2] it is a clearinghouse for ingenious ideas that will keep you abreast of current developments in office[3] systems and procedures.

Mr. Allan Kelly, the manager of our new center, and his well-qualified[4] staff are ready to help you solve your problems in systems analysis and to answer any questions you have[5] about our equipment.

At the center you will see demonstrations of the newest systems, procedures, and machines.[6]

Why not come in soon. Yours very truly, [128]

415 Dear Mr. Gray: Thank you for

your inquiry about Wilson electric postage meters. We manufacture eight[1] different models; they are described in the enclosed booklet. All our models are approved by the Postal Service.[2] The model in which we think you will be interested is the No. 1161 that is pictured and described[3] on page 16. It is a small, self-contained unit that should be completely satisfactory for an office[4] that sends out about 100 letters a week. As you will notice, it sells for $180.[5]

We will be glad to have our representative demonstrate the Model 1161 electric postage[6] meter to you in your office. Please tell us on the enclosed self-addressed postcard when it will be convenient for[7] him to call. Yours very truly,　　[146]

416 Dear Mr. Bruce: In yesterday's *Times* I read that you will soon open an electrical appliance store in Nashville.[1] If you have a position open for a sales representative in your new store, I would like to apply[2] for it.

For the past five years I have been employed as a representative of the National Products Company[3] in Clinton. However, Nashville is my home, and I prefer to work there.

For the National Products Company[4] I successfully sold radios, television sets, and tape recorders; consequently, I feel that I[5] can do a good job for you.

A personal data sheet is enclosed. After you have studied it, I hope you will[6] be kind enough to grant me an interview. Sincerely yours,　　[131]

417 Dear Mr. Gates: The Cunningham electronic calculator we ordered from you on Monday, March 13, was[1] delivered to us yesterday. When our equipment superintendent, Mr. Rice, uncrated the *machine*,° he[2] found that it had been damaged. He found that the automatic accumulator key did not work and that the memory[3] clear key was out of order.

We would appreciate it, Mr. Gates, if you would send us a replacement[4] as soon as possible. Also, please tell us what disposition you want us to make of the defective machine.[5] Sincerely yours,　　[102]
Also correct:
°calculator

LESSON 50

420 *Office Landscaping*

When weeds, crabgrass, and overgrown shrubs run you out of your yard, it is time to do some landscaping. Basically,[1] the same idea applies to a person's home away from home—the office. When noise, drabness, and lack of space interfere[2] with efficiency, management must deal with the situation.

Many companies today are turning[3] to indoor landscaping—using metal, wood, carpeting, and a touch of greenery—in their solution. Though[4] certainly not a new concept, office landscaping has become popular with office designers.

What does landscaping[5] an office entail? A design research company is first commissioned to conduct a study of work and[6] communications patterns. Based on their findings, the designers critically view space, sound, and color. Only then do[7] they lay out a new arrangement.

Basically, landscaping is the arrangement of work areas in[8] private or semiprivate movable clusters to facilitate communications.

Sound control is vital[9] in the well-landscaped office. Distracting noise of machinery, voices, and equipment must be kept to a[10] minimum.

Color is another important consideration. Bright colors add vitality to the work station,[11] but they may also become tiring.

Because landscaping means literally breaking down the old walls of the[12] cell-office concept, the change creates many new problems. The first is one of economics. Will the result be[13] worth the cost of conversion? Some say office landscaping will produce a minimum gain in efficiency of[14] 20 to 30 percent. This is certainly considerable.

Most people about to move into a landscaped[15] office are skeptical. Actually, however, landscaped interiors have proved to be comfortable[16] and efficient in many business situations. [330]—Adapted from *Today's Secretary.*

421 Secretarial Work

Secretarial work is not primarily glamorous; it is difficult. If you work hard, however, a[1] secretarial position is one of importance and responsibility.

The person who wants to progress[2] in the secretarial field should acquire a thorough knowledge of the company's routine and should develop[3] a certain amount of initiative after she has come to know both her job and her boss thoroughly. In[4] return for this hard work, she will get an "extra education." She will gain a firsthand knowledge of a business;[5] in addition, she will have a chance to meet interesting and important people who come to do business with[6] her boss.

As a future secretary, how do you fit into the following personality framework?

Adaptability.[7] Remember that you will be hired to help your employer do his job more efficiently. Thus[8] you must willingly cooperate and take directions, correction, and even criticism.

Personal Conduct.[9] To be a competent secretary, you must maintain a businesslike attitude, never overstepping[10] the employer-employee relationship.

Personal Appearance. Your personal appearance is a vital[11] factor, for your boss must look at you as well as work with you. Select clothes that are conservative but in good style[12] and color.

The opportunities available to secretaries are many and varied. Make the most of[13] your time while you are in school so that you will be able to prepare yourself better for the position of secretary.[14]   [280]

422 Dear Mr. Kelly: Before you refurnish your office, take a tour through our showrooms, where we have 24[1] completely furnished room settings planned by our design staff.

There you will see exactly what your office will look like before[2] you purchase anything. If in those 24 settings you do not see something you like, our interior[3] designers will create an office especially for you.

You need no appointment. Just come in, and one of our[4] representatives will show you our 24 settings and answer all your questions. You will be placing yourself[5] under no obligation. Yours very truly,   [109]

423 Dear Mr. Gray: Would you like to increase your understanding of optical scanning? You can do this by subscribing[1] to the *Optical Scanning Journal*. This journal is published every three weeks and is mailed by first-class mail[2] in order to keep you up to date on all the latest developments in this exciting field.

As an inducement,[3] we are offering you the next six issues of the *Optical Scanning Journal* at the special price of only[4] $9.50. If we receive your order by March 15, we will also send you a free copy of[5] our 64-page booklet, *Optical Scanning in Business*.

To make yourself an expert on optical scanning,[6] fill out and mail the enclosed form. When we receive it, we will send you a copy of *Optical Scanning in Business*[7] and bill you $9.50 for your special subscription to the *Optical Scanning Journal*. Cordially[8] yours,   [161]

424 Dear Mr. Green: Because our organization manufactures nothing but stock tabulating forms, we are able[1] to offer you three major benefits:

1. Prompt deliveries
2. Low prices
3. A guarantee of fine[2] quality

To induce you to try our service, we are making you a special introductory offer. On[3] your first order for stock tabulating forms, we will give you a 10 percent discount, regardless of the size of[4] your order.

Send us your first order today. You have nothing to lose and everything to gain. Very truly yours,[5]
      [100]

Chapter 11

LESSON 51

427 Dear Mr. Fox: Mr. Paul Worth of your accounting department recently told me of a sales vacancy in[1] your organization. I understand that the position involves calling on clients in the states of Florida,[2] Georgia, and South Carolina.

I have had five years' experience in the marketing department of the[3] Federal Department Store, and I have enjoyed my work there. However, I would like a position where I would[4] be able to work outside. The opportunity to call on clients in three southern states is particularly[5] appealing to me.

Enclosed is a data sheet giving information concerning my experience and[6] education. May I come in for an interview soon? Sincerely yours,
      [133]

428 Dear Mr. Gates: If your employees lack enthusiasm for their jobs, make available to them copies of[1] our book, *How to Get the Most Out of Your Job.*

Mr. Harry Smith, the author, has had many years of business[2] experience and has learned to analyze the employment picture from the standpoint of the employee and the[3] employer.

Mr. Smith's book helps your employment situation in the following ways:

1. It speaks to all workers[4] in a language that they can understand.

2. It substitutes an outsider's opinion for a "lecture" from the[5] boss.

3. It urges people to develop the right attitude toward their work, their fellow employees, and their[6] company.

If you provide each of your employees with a copy of this helpful book, you will reap rich dividends.[7] We are sending you a complimentary copy, Mr. Gates, for your personal review. Sincerely yours, [158]

429 Dear Mr. Green: Thank you for sending me a complimentary review copy of your book, *How to Get the Most Out[1] of Your Job.* I have read it carefully and am very much impressed with the well-planned presentation that the author[2] makes.

Please send us 25 copies of the book. We will place these books in our company library for our[3] employees to read in their leisure time. Our training officer plans to hold a series of seminars with our[4] employees after they have all had an opportunity to read the book.

Your bill should be sent to Mr. C.[5] C. Casey, treasurer of Wilson and Company. Please be sure to deduct the 25 percent discount for[6] which we are eligible. Sincerely yours, [128]

430 Dear Mr. Burns: It is a pleasure to tell you that at its meeting yesterday the board of education approved[1] my recommendation that you be employed in our school next year to teach biology. Your salary will be[2] $8,000 for the ten months of the school year.

As we discussed at your interview, your teaching assignment[3] will consist of five classes, two in botany and three in zoology.

The staff members who met you during[4] your interview feel that you are well qualified for this position, and all of us will be pleased to have you join[5] our faculty.

Enclosed are two copies of our regular contract. Please sign one copy and return it to us[6] by April 1; the other copy is for your files. Very truly yours, [133]

431 Dear Mr. Farmer: Your letter telling me that the position of assistant sales manager of the Wilson[1] Company has been filled naturally came as a disappointment to me. I had hoped that the position would[2] be offered to me on the basis of my qualifications and my experience.

I am grateful to you,[3] however, for the time you spent with me in my interview and for the tour of your facilities.

Should another[4] position on your sales force open up in the near future, I would appreciate the opportunity[5] of applying for it. Yours very truly, [108]

432 Dear Mr. James: Thank you for your offer of a position in the accounting department of Fox and Company.[1] Normally, I would have been elated to receive your offer, for I would have enjoyed working for such a[2] progressive, friendly company. Unfortunately, I must decline for personal reasons.

My mother was advised[3] by her doctor to move to a dry climate. We are, therefore, moving to Phoenix next month.

I wish Fox and[4] Company every success in the future. Sincerely yours, [90]

433 Gentlemen: Your agency recommended Miss Linda Jones to us five years ago, and we are grateful for your[1] recommendation. She has been one of the most capable, productive young women in our organization.[2]

Unfortunately, she has just resigned to accept a *position** in New Orleans. We would like you to assist[3] us once again in finding the right person for the job she has left vacant.

The position requires a young person[4] who *possesses*† the following qualifications: a minimum of two years' office experience, good[5] skill in shorthand and typewriting, and a pleasing personality. We are particularly interested in[6] a person who has a good background in English, for he will be asked to do a great deal of creative writing.[7]

If you have someone to suggest,

please telephone me. I will then arrange an interview. Very truly yours, [159]

Also correct:
*job
†has

LESSON 52

438 Dear Mr. Wall: Mr. J. R. Moore, who has been our representative in Detroit during the past three years, will[1] not be able to call on you for several months. As you may know, Mr. Moore's health has not been good for some time. On[2] the advice of his physician, he is taking a three-month leave of absence. We are sure that when he returns, he[3] will give you the same efficient, dependable service that he has given you in the past.

In the meantime, a[4] temporary representative, Mr. Richard Riley, will take Mr. Moore's place. If you need any merchandise[5] before Mr. Riley can call on you, please send us your orders by mail. We will, of course, fill them promptly.[6] Several order blanks are enclosed for your convenience. Sincerely yours, [132]

439 Dear Mr. Jackson: This letter will confirm that Mr. Joseph Rogers was employed as a foreman in our[1] Milwaukee plant for the past four years.

Mr. Rogers performed his job competently, and we regret that circumstances[2] beyond his control made it necessary for him to make his permanent home in New York.

It is a pleasure[3] to recommend

Mr. Rogers for employment in your organization. He is the kind of person who[4] performs his job well and cooperates with his fellow employees. Sincerely yours, [95]

440 Dear Mr. Shaw: For the past four years I have been serving in the Air Force in the office of the chief accountant[1] at the Kelly Air Force Base in San Antonio. When my military service is completed on November[2] 8, I would like to return to my former job with your organization.

As your records will show, I was[3] employed in the accounting department for two years before I was inducted into the Air Force.

It was my[4] understanding at that time that my position would be available to me when I had completed my[5] military service. It will be a pleasure to resume my work with your firm. Sincerely yours, [117]

441 Dear Mr. Baird: Yes, your position with our company will be waiting for you when you are discharged from the Air[1] Force. We are delighted that you will soon be returning to our company.

As you will recall, Mr. Duffy[2] is the senior accountant in our department. However, he will be moving to North Dakota the first of[3] the year; consequently, we will be appointing a new head of that department. You will certainly be one of[4] those we will want to consider for this position.

Please complete the enclosed form so that we can bring your personnel[5] records up to date. Sincerely yours, [107]

442 Dear Mr. Mitchell: I am happy to answer your request for my opinion of Mr. Harold Reed.

As you[1] have already seen his permanent file in the placement department, you know that Mr. Reed had a fine record[2] in college. He was in several of my classes, and in addition to making excellent grades, he always showed[3] considerable initiative. He played a prominent part in reorganizing the student council at[4] Wilson College and upon graduation was awarded a medal for outstanding citizenship.

If you[5] should hire Mr. Reed, I believe he will make a substantial contribution to your company. Sincerely yours,[6] [120]

443 To the Staff: As you were informed in my memorandum of January 5, Jane Smith resigned as art director[1] of our two magazines.

I am happy to announce that Miss Smith's successor will be Mary Green, who will assume[2] her responsibilities on January 20.

Mary is a graduate of the National Art[3] School. She has done much creative work that has appeared in several national magazines during the past year.

Mary's[4] appointment is made upon the recommendation of Harry Brown, our editorial director, to[5] whom she will report. James R. Murphy [107]

444 Dear Miss Day: Your letter expressing interest in summer employment in an office in Syracuse has been referred[1] to me.

Enclosed is a list of offices that will be employing one or more college students during June,[2] July, and August.

To apply for one of these *positions,** complete the enclosed application blank and return it[3] to us. Indicate on the blank the three companies for which you would like to work. We will then get in touch with them[4] and arrange for personal interviews.

It is a pleasure, Miss Day, to give you this help in obtaining a summer[5] position. Cordially yours, [106]
Also correct:
*openings

LESSON 53

448 Dear Mr. Kraft: Your letter of application for a position in our sales department just arrived. Thank you[1] for your interest in Southern Enterprises. As you know, we are one of the country's largest manufacturers[2] of chemicals, and we are constantly expanding.

We do have an opening at this time in Jackson Heights,[3] Mississippi. The job involves calling on pharmacists to sell our line of medical supplies.

Your previous[4] experience is ideal for the type of sales work that we have.

Please let us know when it would be convenient for[5] you to come to our local office for an interview. Cordially yours, [113]

449 Dear Miss Kinney: If you are looking for a job with excitement and glamour, why not consider working for[1] Part-Time, Incorporated. Our organization supplies secretaries, stenographers, and typists on a[2] temporary basis to businesses throughout the country.

Your work will never be monotonous. You will probably[3] work in several different offices for several different employers each year. In addition, you will have the[4] opportunity to live in different parts of the country if you choose to do so.

If your skills are reasonably[5] good and you are a diligent worker, you will probably be able to pass our employment test with flying[6] colors.

Resolve to break the old habit of going to the same job every day. Get out of the rut. Apply[7] for an exciting position with Part-Time, Incorporated today. Cordially yours, [156]

450 Dear Mr. Case: Graduation at East High School is only two months away. Once again, many of the seniors[1] in my classes have made plans to go to college and are thinking about ways to earn the money they will need to[2] meet their expenses.

This year I am particularly eager to help Mary Bradley, an exceptionally[3] bright student who has an excellent scholarship record. She would like to obtain a part-time job in Trenton while[4] she is going to college.

Mary will be a graduate of our business department, where she studied shorthand,[5] typewriting, and office procedures. She can take dictation at 120 words a minute and can type[6] 70 words a minute.

She has a pleasant, cheerful personality and would be a most cooperative[7] team member for your staff.

Please let me know if you would like Mary to come to see you for an interview. A stamped,[8] addressed envelope is enclosed for your convenience in replying. Sincerely yours, [175]

451 Dear Mr. Robertson: Thank you for telling us about Mary Bradley, who is interested in working part[1] time while she is attending Central College here in Trenton. We are always looking for part-time employees with[2] good stenographic skills to help solve our stenographic shortage. As you will recall, we have hired several of your[3] students in the past, all of whom have done an exceedingly fine job for us.

Please ask Miss Bradley to come in to[4] see us as soon as she arrives in Trenton. I am sure we will have a place for her in our organization.[5] Sincerely yours, [103]

452 Dear Mrs. Harper: Thank you for your letter indicating an interest in working in our purchasing department.[1] We do have a vacancy in that department at the present time, and we would indeed be happy to[2] interview you.

If it is convenient, please come to our office on Monday, June 17, at 2 p.m. to discuss[3] the job further. Sincerely yours, [67]

453 Dear Mr. Davis: Wilson Associates has four immediate openings for legal secretaries. These[1] positions require a high school education and two or three years of experience in a lawyer's office. The[2] candidates should be able to type 60 words a minute and write shorthand at 100 words a minute.

The[3] people who are hired will work in a friendly atmosphere and receive generous fringe benefits.

If you have[4] any people on your lists who meet our qualifications and who would be interested in these positions, please[5] have them call me for an appointment at 115-1188 between 3 and 5 p.m. on any Monday[6] or Friday. Yours very truly, [127]

454 Dear Miss Fox: It is quite unlikely that we will have an opening in our office for an accountant within[1] the next few months. We do, however, have an opening for a stenographer.

If you are interested in[2] applying for this position, please do the following things:

1. Complete the enclosed application blank and return[3] it to us in the enclosed stamped, self-addressed envelope.

2. Ask two *persons** familiar with your qualifications[4] to submit letters of recommendation.

3. Arrange for a personal interview by calling our[5] personnel office at 116-1188.

We look forward to receiving your application, Miss Fox. Yours[6] very truly, [123]

Also correct:
*people

LESSON 54

458 Dear Mr. Nelson: As Mr. Hastings probably told you, there is an opening in our firm for an assistant[1] accountant. Mr. Hastings wrote me that you will graduate from college on June 20. He enclosed a record[2] of your grades in the courses you took in college. Your record is very impressive, and you seem to meet the[3] qualifications for our job perfectly.

If you are interested in applying for this position, please[4] fill out the enclosed application form and make an appointment with my secretary to come in to see me.[5] Yours very truly, [104]

a salesman to sell your home furnishings[1] in Tennessee, Kentucky, and Ohio interests me very much.

As I have had three years of[2] experience selling home furnishings, I feel that I am well qualified for this position. My previous selling[3] experience was in Michigan and Minnesota, but since I must move to Kentucky, I would like to be[4] considered a candidate for the position in your organization.

May I come in for an interview[5] at your convenience? Sincerely yours, [107]

459 Dear Sir: Applications are now being accepted for an excellent position for a dynamic salesman[1] with the Empire Products Company, one of the world's largest manufacturers of home furnishings. Only men[2] who have had experience selling home furnishings will be considered.

This is an opportunity for a[3] salesman to become affiliated with a business that is well established and expanding rapidly. Our[4] nationally advertised line of products is one of the finest in the world.

The territory that our new[5] salesman will be covering embraces Tennessee, Kentucky, and Ohio. His headquarters will be either[6] in Lexington or Louisville. He will spend approximately 30 weeks a year traveling; the remaining[7] weeks of the year he will spend in the home office.

If you are interested and qualified for this position,[8] please get in touch with us. Sincerely yours, [167]

460 Dear Mr. Ford: Your letter indicating that you have a vacancy for

461 Dear Mr. Wade: We were pleased to receive your letter and learn of your interest in one of the openings on our[1] sales staff.

We suggest that you come to our office for an interview sometime during the week of June 12. Our[2] employment office conducts interviews on Monday, Tuesday, and Wednesday mornings. Sincerely yours, [57]

462 Dear Miss White: The study you are making regarding a secretary's duties and qualifications impresses[1] us very much. We are happy to give you all the information we have available.

Enclosed are three[2] booklets that were prepared by our staff. Also enclosed is an article written by our personnel director,[3] Mr. A. C. Bentley, which was published in last month's issue of our company magazine. It will give you[4] a pretty good idea of our training program.

I hope this information will be of help to you. If there is[5] any further information you would like, please feel free to write us.

When you have completed your study, we would[6] appreciate receiving a copy. Cordially yours, [130]

463 To the Staff: Beginning August 2, representatives of the Wilson Moving Company will conduct a survey[1] of all furniture, equipment, and other material that is to be moved to our new building on Fifth[2] Avenue.

During the two weeks that the survey will be in progress, it will be necessary for these[3] representatives to enter every one of our offices, storerooms, and closets. The data that they collect will be[4] of great importance in planning our move. Therefore, I ask every one of you to cooperate with these[5] representatives. I know that you will find them to be friendly, courteous, and businesslike. J. C. Willis [118]

464 To All Department Managers: Recently you received from the personnel department a booklet describing[1] the conference they are planning on office procedures for new employees. I encourage you to have those[2] employees who have joined our staff during the past year in clerical or secretarial capacities to[3] attend this conference.

Also, if you have employees who have been with us for more than a year but who could benefit[4] from this type of conference, ask them to attend. James C. Green [91]

465 Dear Dr. Washington: The Wilson Furniture Company will be happy to send a representative to[1]

the State College campus on Friday, June 6, to conduct interviews for your spring graduates.

We will be[2] interviewing applicants in the *fields** of accounting, management, and office administration.

We would appreciate[3] it if you would schedule these interviews for your students. Each student should be assigned a 30-minute session[4] with our interviewer. The first interview should *begin†* at 9:00 a.m., and the last interview should be scheduled[5] to begin no later than 4:30 p.m.

We would appreciate it if each candidate would complete one[6] of the enclosed application blanks before the interview.

We look forward to employing a number of your[7] graduates. Sincerely yours, [145]
Also correct:
*areas
†start

LESSON 55

468 *The Job Hunt*

Do you have the jitters about getting that first job? Well, almost everybody does—and with good cause.[1] Work is important to us because we spend almost half of each 24-hour weekday getting ready for work,[2] getting to work, working, and unwinding from work. If a job means so much, then you should exercise a great deal of[3] care in selecting your first one.

Naturally, if you haven't yet held

a job, you won't know what it is about[4] a job that makes it particularly right for you. But if you ask yourself a few questions before you launch your[5] campaign, you will at least have an idea.

Write down the answers to these questions: What do I like to do? What are[6] my abilities? What courses have I taken that will help me on the job? What work experience have I had?[7] What beginning salary do I want?

In launching your secretarial career, you will have to be your own[8] secretary first. For job hunting, you will need a stack of 3 by 5 cards and a calendar. Each time you make a[9] contact, record all vital information on a card: name of agency or company, address, phone number,[10] your source of referral, interviewer, and the date of the contact.

Another secretarial job that you[11] should perform for yourself is the compilation of a personal file. Besides your data sheet and carbon copies[12] of your letters of application, the file should include several permanent letters of reference from people,[13] excluding relatives, who know your work abilities and can vouch for your good character.

If you do your job[14] hunting with care, there is no reason why you shouldn't have more than one good offer. Don't grab the first job that comes along;[15] be selective. It is impossible for you to predict how well a particular job will turn out for[16] you, but if you know how to question yourself and the job and if you have prepared yourself properly, there is no[17] reason why you

and your first job shouldn't be a perfect match. [351] Adapted from *Today's Secretary*

469 *Selling Yourself*

The hardest thing you ever have to sell in your lifetime is yourself.

To win any job, you must[1] beat the competition. This is a particularly difficult task, especially when you apply in writing[2] for a job. Inevitably, the bulk of written matter from job hunters is filed for "future" reference—the[3] very distant future. A total of 346 men answered an ad not long ago; only[4] 11 of them were invited for personal interviews.

There are three ways to apply for a job in writing:[5] by filling out a formal application, by preparing a personal history, and by writing a letter.[6]

The Formal Application. Application blanks are almost as standard as office desks. They ask pretty much[7] the same questions. When you fill out the application, remember that brevity, completeness, and neatness are[8] important. Answer every question asked, and make the answers short.

The Personal History. The material that[9] goes into a personal history is not too different from that which goes into a formal job-application[10] blank. On the personal history, however, you have more opportunity to present your qualifications[11] in a favorable light. Your summary should be short and clear. Get it on one or two typewritten pages[12] if possible. List your jobs in reverse order, starting with the present job and working backward. If you are a[13] student and have held no previous positions, say so.

You should tell exactly how you qualify for the job[14] for which you are applying. Specify what you can offer the job—and forget what the job might offer you. From[15] your total education and experience, point to those things that have direct application to the position[16] in which you are interested.

Your personal-history summary should be attached to any[17] application blanks you fill out. If your first contact is an interview, leave the summary with the person who interviews[18] you.

The Letter. It is a good idea to cover a job application with a letter if you are[19] submitting the application by mail. The main rule is to make the letter short and to the point. You should say, in[20] a line or two, what the most important single fact is that qualifies you for the job and then refer your reader[21] to the other documents for the details.

Remember, it is *you* that you are selling. A buyer is there[22] if you know how to interest him in the merits of your product.   [452]

Chapter 12

LESSON 56

472 Dear Sir: If you have not yet seen our new book, *Advertising in Today's Business,* you have a treat in store for you.[1] This book is the most complete guide to advertising ever published. The author, John Worth, is a recognized leader[2] in the field, and he has presented his thoughts in a clear, concise manner.

Advertising in Today's Business[3] is a perfect book for your own library. It will also make an ideal present for a friend.

Send for a copy[4] today. If you are not thoroughly satisfied with it, you may return it to us and pay nothing. We are[5] sure, however, that you will be so pleased with it that you will not only keep your copy but will also order[6] several others for your friends. Sincerely yours,   [127]

473 Dear Mr. Ball: Your name has been given to us as an author in the field of advertising. We would like to[1] invite you to prepare an article for publication in our magazine, *Advertising Week.*

We are looking[2] for articles on the effects of advertising on children's television programs, and we understand[3] that you have done some research in this area. We believe our readers would like to know what effect advertising[4] directed chiefly at the preschool market has on sales of products made for children.

If you would like to[5] submit such an article, will you please send us a manuscript by December 1. It should contain approximately[6] 2,000 words. We will plan to publish it sometime in the spring.

We look forward to hearing from you.[7] Sincerely yours,   [141]

474 Dear Mr. Holmes: Thank you

for your invitation to write an article for *Advertising Week*. I am happy[1] to accept this invitation, and I will submit my manuscript before December 1.

The title of my[2] article will be *Children's Advertising—Yes or No.*

Thank you for the opportunity to write for your[3] magazine. Sincerely yours,　　　　　　　　　　　[64]

475 Dear Mr. Smith: Are office expenses giving you gray hair? If they are, we have an answer to your problem—Frank[1] Baker's book, *How to Cut Office Overhead.* This book lists 400 ways in which you can cut your costs.

The book[2] emphasizes what most businessmen overlook—the fact that every dollar saved in office expenses is a direct[3] contribution to company profit. You do not have to increase sales in order to increase profits; just[4] reduce office expenses!

Why not send today for a copy of *How to Cut Office Overhead.* We will send[5] it to you at once on a ten-day trial basis. If you like the book, you can send us a check for $6;[6] if you don't, simply return the book.

Use the enclosed card to place your order. Yours very truly, [137]

476 Dear Mr. Miller: People often juggle their birthdays a bit, and the dates of some holidays vary from year[1] to year. You can be sure, though, that Christmas will come on December 25, and that date is rapidly approaching.[2]

Have you entered your Christmas renewal gift order for *Mystery Magazine* for your friends yet?

As you know,[3] this magazine is the ideal gift for a friend who lives far away as well as for "the person who has[4] everything." *Mystery Magazine* brings many hours of entertaining, electrifying reading.

If you have sent[5] us your Christmas list, thank you very much. If you haven't, why not use the enclosed gift form to place your order now.[6]

The enclosed stamped envelope will speed your order to us. You need not pay now; we will send a bill after the[7] holidays. Cordially yours,
　　　　　　　　　　　[144]

477 Dear Mr. West: We are sure that you wish to keep up with current newspaper articles. They are indispensable[1] to you in your business.

Through the use of our press clipping service, you will be able to keep in touch with the[2] press comments that are *useful** to you in your business. Our service is economical, and it covers all major[3] newspapers in the country.

If you will stop to consider the vast amount of time and effort you would have[4] to spend searching through newspapers for items of interest, you will realize what a substantial saving our service[5] represents. Why not join the many subscribers who *benefit†* from this service today, Mr. West. Cordially[6] yours,　　　　　　　　　[121]
Also correct:
*helpful
†profit

LESSON 57

482 Dear Mr. Russell: Thank you for your order for our No. 1302 offset press. You are making an[1] investment that will pay fine dividends in the future.

As you may know, this model has been on the market for only[2] a few months. We knew that it would be well received by printers who are interested in cutting costs, but we[3] did not foresee how big the demand would be.

The demand has been so great that it will take us two or three months to[4] fill your order. We are sorry for the delay, Mr. Russell.

We assure you that we will deliver and install[5] your press as soon as possible. We know you will be pleased with it once you place it in operation. Yours very[6] truly,   [122]

483 Dear Mr. Ray: Mr. Joseph West is being considered for the position of editor in our trade book[1] division. We understand that Mr. West was employed by your publishing company in Framingham for several[2] years.

We would appreciate it, therefore, if you would complete and return the enclosed questionnaire concerning[3] Mr. West. If you have any additional information that you feel would be of help to us as we[4] consider him for this position, we hope you will let us have it.

Thank you for your cooperation. Sincerely[5] yours,   [101]

484 Dear Mr. Jones: I am happy to be able to give you a favorable report on Mr. Joseph West.[1] The completed questionnaire is enclosed.

Mr. West was on our staff for five years. When he joined our organization,[2] he was an assistant editor in charge of our history, geography, and science programs; later[3] he was appointed senior editor.

Mr. West is a very competent worker. He is a man of[4] integrity and has a delightful, pleasing personality. It is a pleasure to give him an unqualified[5] recommendation. I am confident that he will be a valuable addition to your staff.

Please let[6] me know if I can provide you any other information. Sincerely yours,   [135]

485 Dear Mr. Wilson: We were delighted to receive the manuscript for your new book, *Economics Today*. Our[1] editorial committee has studied the manuscript, and all our editors agree that it is a complete,[2] well-organized piece of work.

We should be able to complete the editorial work in two or three months[3] and have the book on the market sometime next year.

Congratulations on the fine job you have done. Sincerely yours,[4]   [80]

486 Dear Mrs. Grace: A child's learning day doesn't end with the ringing of a bell in school. It continues at home with[1] every research paper he writes, every project he prepares, and every examination he studies for.

This[2] can be a difficult task for children, but the *American Book of Knowledge* can make things a little easier.[3] This book is designed for students. It is written in language that is easy to understand.

The *American*[4] *Book of Knowledge* encourages deeper investigation and independent research.

Place the *American*[5] *Book of Knowledge* at the disposal of your children. You will be making a priceless investment. Cordially[6] yours, [121]

487 Dear Mrs. Bates: Nothing is ever so good that it cannot be improved, and that includes *Wilson's Basic Reader.*[1] The new sixth edition is even better than the fifth for these reasons:

1. We have profited by the feedback[2] we received from users of the fifth edition.

2. We have adopted many suggestions from teachers using[3] other materials.

3. We have had our materials reviewed by several well-known reading consultants.

4.[4] We have added many teaching and learning options to suit the needs and abilities of all teachers and students.[5]

Wilson's Basic Reader has always been better than most other readers; now it is better than ever.

For[6] an examination copy of *Wilson's Basic Reader,* fill out and return the enclosed card. Sincerely yours,[7] [140]

488 Dear Mr. Drake: The guest editorial by Harvey Smith that appeared in the Sunday edition of the *Times*[1] is, in my opinion, highly improper. A *person** who writes an editorial attacking the principles[2] of our organization shows his disregard for our basic beliefs.

Our organization has never[3] tried to achieve growth for the sake of growth alone. We have always looked for quality rather than quantity in[4] our membership.

I am now *preparing*† an editorial refuting Mr. Smith's statements about our[5] organization, and I hope you will publish it in next Sunday's edition of the *Times.* Sincerely yours, [118]

Also correct:
*individual, man
†writing

LESSON 58

492 Dear Mr. Jones: Our company is planning to publish a handbook on telephone techniques for our secretarial[1] and clerical employees, and we would like to have your assistance. As a representative of the[2] telephone company, you can give us valuable guidance in the preparation of this handbook.

We want[3] our handbook to cover both the technical and human relations aspects of telephone usage.

If you are[4] free one day next week, we would like to arrange a conference to discuss this project with you. Would Friday, May 15,[5] be a convenient time for you? Cordially yours, [109]

493 Dear Mr. Deems: We deeply appreciate the favorable comments you made in reference to our publication,[1] *The Office Employee,* in your letter of April 16. We have great confidence in our editorial[2] staff and take great pride in its performance.

As you requested, we are sending you several back issues[3] of *The Office Employee*. We are also placing your name on our mailing list to receive future copies.

We[4] hope, Mr. Deems, that the material in our magazine will prove interesting and helpful to you. Cordially[5] yours,　　　　[101]

494 Dear Mr. Morse: We are pleased to announce the publication of the fifth edition of *Business Management*. This[1] textbook provides a basic foundation for understanding the role of management in the modern business world.[2]

Business Management deals with the planning, organizing, and controlling functions of business in the light of the[3] latest research in both human resources and technology.

We believe that this book will make an important[4] contribution to your courses in business administration.

If you will return the enclosed card, we will send[5] you an examination copy. Sincerely yours,　　[109]

495 Mr. Wolff: We were very much disturbed to learn that some of the schools using our new book, *Modern Communications*,[1] have complained that the covers were breaking. We immediately stopped production on the book in order to[2] have the binder run a series of tests on the cover.

After conducting exhaustive tests on the cover, the[3] binder could find nothing wrong. We have, therefore, instructed him to resume production of the book.

I think it would[4] be a good idea to ask one of the schools that have complained to send us several copies of the defective[5] book. The binder will then be able to determine exactly how the books were defective and what remedial[6] action, if any, is necessary. A. J. Green　　　[130]

496 Dear Mr. James: I would like to send you a complimentary copy of *Getting Ahead in Business*, one of the[1] most stimulating booklets ever published.

Mature men who seek a better understanding of business fundamentals[2] will appreciate the booklet's simple approach to the problems they face every day. They will welcome its[3] explanation of our executive training program, which was prepared by our staff in cooperation with[4] scores of executives.

There is no charge for *Getting Ahead in Business* simply because it is worth only what[5] you make it worth. Some men glance through it and toss it aside. Others have found a fortune in its pages. Its appeal,[6] naturally, is limited to ambitious men who are not content to remain in their present income brackets.[7]

I want you to decide for yourself whether or not *Getting Ahead in Business* is intended for you. If[8] you feel that it is, please feel free to send for your copy today. A postcard is enclosed for your convenience. Yours[9] truly,　　　　[181]

497 To the Staff: I am pleased to

announce that the Meade Publishing Company will soon open a bookstore in the Wilson[1] Building in Washington. The store will be located on the main floor with a large window opening on[2] Constitution Avenue.

It will be approximately the size of our New York store and will carry books of all[3] publishers. It will be under the direction of James Baker, vice president in charge of all bookstore operations.[4] The manager of the store will be Eileen Smith. Harry K. Barnes [92]

498 Mr. Green: As you suggested, I asked the California Community College, one of the schools that complained[1] about the cover of *Modern Communications*, to send me six of the books that were defective. Those books[2] arrived, and I am *sending°* them to you.

When you receive them, you will notice that the binding on them has cracked.

I[3] hope that you will be able to determine what is causing this problem and correct it without delay. If the[4] problem is not solved quickly, we may have difficulty *marketing†* this book in the future. A. R. Wolff [99]

Also correct:
°shipping, mailing
†selling

LESSON 59

502 Dear Dr. Taylor: Thank you for sending me a copy of your research report, "Shorthand Writers in Today's Business[1] World." Our publication committee has reviewed your manuscript, and I am happy to report that it voted[2] to publish it.

As you probably are aware, we have a backlog of manuscripts that have been approved for[3] publication. Because of the timeliness of your subject, however, we are scheduling it for publication[4] in the May issue of the *Journal*. Our editorial board feels that there is justification for giving[5] high priority to a research report such as yours.

Having formerly been a member of the faculty[6] of the business department of Wilson High School, I am delighted to learn from the results of your research[7] that the demand for stenographers is increasing each year. Sincerely yours, [154]

503 Dear Mrs. Maxwell: Your payment for your subscription to *Home Magazine* is now past due. We assume, Mrs. Maxwell,[1] that this is merely an oversight. All you have to do to continue receiving *Home Magazine* is to[2] fill out the enclosed form and return it to me. The envelope doesn't even need a stamp; we will pay the postage.[3]

Don't put it off; get your order in the mail today. With so many excellent recipes and menus coming[4] in future issues to make your food budget stretch, we are sure you wouldn't want to miss a single issue of[5] *Home Magazine*. Sincerely yours, [106]

504 Gentlemen: Today I received a statement for $7 for the Christmas gift subscription I placed with you[1] on December 2. As your records will show, I asked you to send one gift subscription to Mr. Paul Pine, 1405[2] East Street, Denver, Colorado 88202. Your advertising folder says that one subscription[3] costs $4 and that two subscriptions cost $7.

You have apparently charged me for two subscriptions.[4] I did place an order for two gift subscriptions last year, but this year I ordered just one.

Enclosed is my check for[5] $4. Yours very truly,   [106]

505 Dear Mrs. Pierce: Each month the *Reader's Monthly* supplies more than a million of its subscribers with the best selections[1] from hundreds of leading magazines, journals, and current books.

In order to acquaint you with the quality[2] of the material in the *Reader's Monthly,* we would like to send you a recent issue containing 35[3] selected articles. To obtain your free copy, just sign and return the enclosed postage-paid card.

After[4] you have read the sample issue, we are confident that you will understand why the *Reader's Monthly* enjoys such[5] popularity and that you will want to become a regular subscriber. Yours very truly,   [118]

506 Dear Mr. Henderson: We are planning to publish a paperback edition of our best-selling book,[1] *Personality Development,* and we would like to receive a bid from your company for printing this edition.[2] It will contain 264 pages. We will supply camera copy and artwork for the book. The cover[3] is to be printed in three colors and the inside in one color.

We are sending you additional[4] specifications separately along with a copy of the hardback edition. If you would like to submit[5] a bid on the printing of the paperback edition, please do so on or before August 5. Sincerely yours,[6]   [120]

507 Dear Mr. Harding: Thank you, Mr. Harding, for the opportunity to submit a bid on the printing of[1] the paperback edition of *Personality Development.* Our bid is enclosed.

Please note that our[2] specifications call for reducing the size of the hardback book slightly. By making this modification in size,[3] we can produce the paperback edition at a much lower cost than otherwise.

If you entrust us with the[4] printing of this book, we assure you that you will be highly pleased with the quality of our work as well as with[5] our fast service. Sincerely yours,   [106]

508 Gentlemen: I have just completed my work on a new tax guide that I sincerely believe can be a best seller[1] during the months of February, March, and April, the months in which most taxpayers are filling out their tax[2] forms.

The guide discusses the provisions of the present tax laws in simple language, lists deductions that taxpayers[3] often overlook, and takes the taxpayer step by step through Form 1040. The taxpayer who has *read*°[4] this guide will be able to fill out his own tax form accurately and without difficulty.

If you are[5] interested in publishing this guide, I will be happy to send it to you for review. May I hear from you soon.[6] Sincerely yours,

[123]

Also correct:
*studied

LESSON 60

511 *The Business Letter and Collections*

The business letter is an effective means of inducing delinquent customers to bring their accounts up to[1] date. It lends itself to a diplomatic approach to the collection problem. It is important, therefore, that[2] the writer have a proper understanding of the whole idea behind credits and collections. He should think of[3] overdue accounts as customers of the company who have helped to make the business a success and whose[4] patronage it is desirable to retain.

Each company must establish its own policy with regard to[5] the application of the collection system. There are varying factors and problems in the operation[6] of different types of businesses, and these involve a variation in procedure. The collection system[7] involves the sending of statements, formal notification letters, and personal letters. The latter part of[8] the series uses appeals to the honor, pride, fairness, or self-interest of the customer. These appeals are[9] called the heart of the collection letter. If they are adapted to the customer, they frequently bring either[10] a payment or a frank response from the customer.

When a customer does not respond to any of the[11] conventional procedures, sometimes the "stunt letter" is particularly effective. This type of letter bases[12] its appeal on an unusual idea and on a cheerful approach to the problem. The application of[13] the stunt idea requires imagination on the part of the writer. However, when the idea presented[14] in the letter does capture the fancy of the debtor, it can be very effective. It is also important[15] that the creditor organization exert care not to embarrass the customer or hurt his feelings[16] in any way.

[323]

512 *The Business Letter and Adjustments*

There are many reasons why customers have cause for complaint against a business. They receive discourteous treatment,[1] they receive the wrong merchandise, or the goods do not measure up to their complete satisfaction. These grievances,[2] whether real or imagined, must be met fairly by the adjustment department. They provide an excellent[3] opportunity to earn the goodwill and understanding of the immediate customer and of the public[4] at large. A store or a business soon becomes known for its fair and considerate dealings.

It is important[5] in writing an adjustment letter to keep in mind the point of view of the person presenting the complaint and[6] to sympathize with his position. The letter should state cheerfully the adjustment action and close with a goodwill[7] statement. Some businesses, such as department stores and mail-order houses, follow the policy that the[8] "customer is always right."

One of the most important principles to remember in handling customer grievances[9] is promptness. When complaints are handled promptly, they remain in their proper perspective. If they are neglected[10] and embarrassment and delay are added to the actual damage, the customer is angered. Loss of the[11] customer's patronage and perhaps even litigation may result. [233]

513 *The Sales Letter*

Direct mail illustrates another very important use of the business letter. Since the sales letter goes out[1] only to prospects who have been placed on a mailing list, it can be a sharpshooting method of sales advertising[2] as opposed to the buckshot method of most other advertising media. Direct mail has the advantage[3] of selectivity. Waste circulation is avoided if the mailing list is carefully checked and kept[4] up to date. [82]

514 Dear Miss Hoffman: Thank you for your order for five copies of our book, *Cooking Can Be Fun.* Before we ship these copies[1] to you, please tell us on the enclosed form which edition we should send you— the leather-bound edition, which sells[2] for $8.50, or the loose-leaf edition, which sells for $6.60. An envelope is[3] also enclosed for your convenience in returning the form to us. Sincerely yours, [76]

Chapter 13

LESSON 61

517 Dear Mr. Austin: Thank you for your letter telling me that you have had an offer of $24,000[1] from James Barnes for my house on Worth Street. Since I would like to settle all my business affairs in the city as[2] soon as possible, I am willing to accept the offer.

As you know, I have to be in Chicago by the[3] first of next month to start work on a new job. It is urgent, therefore, that I complete all the details of the[4] transaction before I leave. I would like to come to your office sometime Tuesday morning, April 10, to sign the[5] necessary papers. Will you please telephone me if this time is not satisfactory. Yours very truly,[6] [120]

518 Dear Mr. Davis: If it is convenient, I would like to come to your office on Monday, March 19, at 9[1] a.m. to discuss a loan for our real estate company. We want to purchase a tract of land on Moon Lake,[2] which is located eight miles from Springfield. In order to do this, we will need to borrow about $100,000.[3]

At the present time this land is undeveloped. We plan, however, to make the following improvements:[4]
1. Divide the land into 24 units.
2. Develop a system of streets.
3. Do selective[5] clearing of the natural forest growth to prepare a housing site for each unit.

When this work is completed,[6] the property will be sold for the development of vacation homes. We believe the market for homes of this[7] type will be good.

Is the time I have suggested convenient? If it is not, please suggest another time. Very[8] truly yours, [162]

519 Dear Mr. Williams: Because of circumstances beyond my control, I will be unable to come to the bank[1] on Monday, June 8, for the conference that we had planned.

I will, however, be able to come on Monday, June[2] 15. Unless I hear from you to the contrary, I will assume that this is a convenient time for you. Sincerely[3] yours, [62]

520 Dear Mr. Turner: Enclosed is a copy of the estimate we have prepared for remodeling your home. We have[1] included the cost of both materials and labor.

As you requested, we have also made a separate[2] estimate on the cost of building an additional bedroom.

If we receive your authorization by June[3] 15, we can start work on your remodeling project on July 1. Assuming that we do not encounter any[4] untoward delays, we should be able to complete the job in three months.

If you have any questions concerning[5] the estimate, please get in touch with us. Sincerely yours, [110]

521 Dear Mr. Dix: You will recall that I had planned to spend Friday, November 6, with you looking at the houses[1] that are available for pur-

chase in Akron. However, I have been asked to attend an all-day business conference[2] on that day; consequently, I cannot keep my appointment with you.

When I return to the office, I[3] will get in touch with you and arrange for another appointment.

I regret any inconvenience this change in[4] my plans may cause you. Very truly yours, [87]

522 Dear Mr. Weaver: In last Sunday's newspaper I saw your advertisement for the house you have for sale on Main[1] Street in Cleveland. According to the ad, this house is located on a large, beautifully landscaped plot.

I am[2] considering the purchase of a home at this time, and I would like to have specific *details** concerning the[3] house and land.

If the property meets my requirements, I will arrange to come to Cleveland to see it. Sincerely[4] yours, [82]

Also correct:
*information, facts

Office-Style Dictation

523 (*As dictated*) Dear Mr. James: I have just learned [no, *heard*] that the five-acre plot on West Street [no, *Avenue*] will be placed on the market in a few days. This plot is in a desirable location. (Scratch out that last sentence.) Because of the desirable location of this piece of land, there will no doubt be many potential buyers as soon as the news is made public [no, *is announced*].

If you are interested in purchasing this piece of land, please call me at

116-1117 as soon as you receive this letter. Sincerely yours,

523 (*As it would be transcribed*) Dear Mr. James: I have just heard that the five-acre plot on West Avenue will be placed on the market in a few[1] days. Because of the desirable location of this piece of land, there will no doubt be many potential buyers[2] as soon as the news is announced.

If you are interested in purchasing this piece of land, please call me at[3] 116-1117 as soon as you receive this letter. Sincerely yours, [74]

LESSON 62

528 Dear Mr. Evans: Thank you for your inquiry about houses in the Philadelphia area. We have[1] one house that might meet your needs. It is a ranch-type in Medford that was placed on the market only a few days ago.[2]

If you would like to see this house, we will be glad to show it to you at any time that is convenient for[3] you. We suggest, however, that you plan to see it as soon as possible because the house is a bargain and[4] may not be on the market long.

When you receive this letter, please call me to let me know whether this house appeals[5] to you. Very truly yours, [105]

529 Dear Mr. Olson: As you know, for the past three years I have lived in your house at 319 Third Avenue. On[1] the whole, I have been very happy with it. However, there are several items that need immediate attention.[2] Here are four things that are wrong:

1. The pressure gauge on the furnace does not operate properly.

2. The[3] electric motor that operates the furnace has been vibrating and discharging smoke.

3. The thermostat that[4] regulates the heat is broken.

4. There is a large hole in the carpeting in the living room that is hazardous.[5]

I will appreciate your prompt attention to these problems. Sincerely yours, [114]

530 Dear Miss Harper: Enclosed is a copy of the signed lease confirming our arrangements for you to rent Apartment[1] 44 in the Ridgewood Building in Billings, Montana. You may take occupancy on October 1.

As[2] the whole responsibility for supervising the apartments in the building rests on us, please let us know[3] when anything needs attention. We are eager to see that the apartments are always in good condition; therefore,[4] we will consider it a favor if you will inform us of any necessary repairs that should be[5] made. Cordially yours, [103]

531 Dear Mr. Gross: In September I will be transferred to our company's main plant in Madison, and I would like to[1] purchase a home somewhere near it.

My family and I plan to come to Madison on Monday, July 10, and[2] we would appreciate it if you would show us several houses. We will need a home with six or seven rooms.[3] We will arrive at your office at 10 a.m.

if this is satisfactory with you. Sincerely yours, [78]

532 Dear Mr. Baker: You have probably heard about Twin Rivers, that beautiful little town in New Jersey. Wouldn't[1] you like to live there? You can rent an apartment there for as little as $170 a[2] month. Your rent includes the use of the swimming and tennis club.

In Twin Rivers you can feel safe day and night because[3] it is protected by its own well-trained police department.

Come out and let us show you the apartments we have[4] available. Call us at 161-1188 to make an appointment at your convenience. Cordially[5] yours, [101]

533 Dear Mr. Smith: We have recently published a valuable little booklet that we want to send you free of[1] charge. It is entitled *Investing Successfully in Real Estate*. This booklet explains why smart investors are[2] buying land now. It mentions some of the best places to buy land today, based on population projections and[3] economic forecasts. It also explains the services that the American Real Estate Company[4] renders to land investors.

To get your copy, simply return the enclosed card. Very truly yours, [98]

534 Dear Mr. Day: The next time you must move, let Davis Movers take care of all the details.

Our men know how to pack[1] and unpack things. They know how to pick things up and how to put things down. Most of our men have been with us a long time.[2] In fact, our men have the longest record of service with one moving company in the moving industry.

So[3] call us when you must make your next move. You will be glad that you did. Sincerely yours, [74]

535 Dear Mr. Morgan: Thank you for letting me know about the problems you are having with the airconditioner[1] in my apartment at 1109 State Street.

After looking through my files, I find that the airconditioner[2] has not been serviced for three years. I usually have all appliances checked every two years, but I forgot[3] to do so last year. I have arranged to have a repairman call at the apartment on Monday morning, April[4] 10, at 10 a.m. He will make all repairs, replacements, and adjustments that are needed.

Please feel free to *call*° me[5] whenever any appliance is not functioning properly. Very truly yours, [115]

Also correct:
°telephone, write

LESSON 63

539 Gentlemen: I will be moving to Troy soon and would like to buy a house with three bedrooms and a playroom. I would[1] prefer a house in the eastern part of the city. Do you have a good listing of available houses in[2] this area? If you do, I would appreciate hearing from you.

If you have any descriptive folders or[3] other advertising materials showing some of these homes, please send them to me. Sincerely yours, [78]

540 Dear Mr. Edwards: Enclosed is a list of the houses in Framingham that we think will meet the requirements of[1] your bookkeeper, Mr. James C. Reed. Our representative in Framingham reports that the housing units checked[2] in red on the list appear to be best suited to Mr. Reed's requirements.

May we suggest that you ask Mr.[3] Reed to write directly to our representative in Framingham, Mr. R. M. Russell. His address and phone[4] number are shown on the attached card. Mr. Russell will be glad to assist the Reeds in every way that he[5] can.

If at any time you have other friends or employees whom we can help locate in either Framingham or[6] in any of the other cities we serve, please do not hesitate to call on us. Sincerely yours, [138]

541 Dear Mr. Young: At the present time, Mr. Young, we actually have only two apartments that will be vacant[1] on October 15. One unit consists of two bedrooms, one bathroom, a living room, and a large kitchen.[2] This apartment rents for $225 a month. The other apartment has three bedrooms, two bathrooms,[3] a living room, and a large kitchen. It rents for $300 a month.

Your letter indicates that you[4] would be willing to pay between $200 and $250 a month; therefore, I believe[5] that the first apartment would be more appropriate for you.

If you think that one of these apartments might meet your[6] needs, may I suggest that you make arrangements to see both of them soon. Apartments are very much in demand in Nashville;[7] therefore, it is unlikely that these apartments will be available long. Sincerely yours, [157]

542 Dear Mr. Draper: As you will recall, last Saturday you showed my family and me a piece of property[1] on the shore of Long Lake. We were very much impressed with the lot you showed us. After considering all the pros[2] and cons carefully, we are satisfied that this lot is the one we want to purchase.

We understand that the price[3] is $4,500. We want to make a $500 down payment and pay the remainder[4] in 40 monthly payments of $100 each.

If it is convenient for you, I will be at your office[5] punctually at 10 a.m. on Tuesday, July 16, to sign the necessary papers. Yours very[6] truly, [121]

543 Dear Mr. White: Tuesday, July 16, at 10 a.m. will be a convenient time for us to meet in my office[1] to discuss the papers involved in the sale of the property on Long Lake.

While it is not absolutely[2] essential, you will be wise to have your attorney look over the papers before you sign them. This will prevent[3] any possible misunderstandings. Sincerely yours, [70]

544 Dear Mr. Paris: We can offer

you for immediate occupancy your choice of more than 20 homes in[1] Green Village.

When you purchase a home in Green Village, you make an investment in gracious living. In Green Village[2] we have 35 acres of land on which you will find two swimming pools, five tennis courts, and many other[3] recreational facilities. Very soon we will even have a shopping center.

Your home is ready and waiting.[4] Come to Green Village and select the home that meets your needs.

For an appointment with a member of our sales staff,[5] simply call us at 679-8900. Very truly yours, [113]

545 Dear Mr. Ryder: A very good friend of mine from Vicksburg recommended your agency to me.

I will soon[1] be moving to Vicksburg, where I plan to work on a project that requires a great deal of historical research.[2] Consequently, I would like to rent an apartment in the vicinity of the Vicksburg Historical[3] Library. Could you recommend an apartment to me?

As I will be writing and studying a good deal of the[4] time, I prefer to *live** in a quiet neighborhood that is within walking distance of the library.

If you[5] know of any apartments that you can show me, please let me know. I will arrange to come to Vicksburg at a time[6] that is mutually convenient. Sincerely yours, [130]
Also correct:
*be

LESSON 64

549 Dear Mr. Harper: A short time ago I joined the staff of the Thomson Realty Company, which has listings[1] throughout the city.

If you or any of your colleagues should have occasion to purchase, sell, or rent local[2] property, perhaps I can be of assistance to you.

I have lived in Pittsburgh for 20 years, and during that time[3] I have become well acquainted with all areas of the city. This experience enables me to give[4] you the best possible service whenever you need a real estate agent. Sincerely yours, [97]

550 Dear Mr. Black: Thank you for your inquiry of Friday, June 6, about the office we have available in[1] the Brownsville Office Building. We can unhesitatingly recommend it to you.

May I suggest that you come[2] to Brownsville during the week of June 22 to see the office. If it is impossible for you to[3] come during that week, please suggest another time that will be satisfactory. I can easily arrange my[4] schedule to suit your convenience. Very truly yours, [90]

551 Dear Mr. Moore: Thank you for your letter concerning the purchase of our home. It is true that our house is for sale,[1] and we will be pleased to show it to you.

We think it is in an ideal location, and it seems to be the[2] proper size to accommodate your family. There are four large bedrooms, two bathrooms, a kitchen, a large dining room,[3] a family room, a living room, and a large basement that can readily be converted into a playroom.[4] The house is located three blocks from an elementary school, four blocks from a high school, and six blocks from the Evansville[5] Shopping Mart. The grounds are appealingly landscaped and need very little work done on them.

If you would like more[6] information about our home, please call me. I hope you will be able to come to Evansville soon to see the[7] house for yourself. Sincerely yours, [146]

552 Dear Mr. Stacy: Thank you for your thoughtfulness in sending me the information I requested about your[1] house.

I will be in Evansville on Saturday, April 15, at which time I would like to see the house. I hope[2] that this date will be convenient for you. If it is not, please call me. Very truly yours, [56]

553 Dear Mr. Harris: We are pleased to learn that you and your family plan to make Greensburg your home. We will be happy[1] to help you find a five-room house that will suit your family's needs and tastes.

Our newest development, Green Springs,[2] is just ten miles south of Greensburg. When the entire project is completed about the middle of June, there will be[3] 50 homes in the development. We have already completed five homes, and they are for sale and ready for[4] occupancy.

Enclosed is a brochure that gives complete details about Green Springs. We hope, Mr. Harris, that we[5]

may soon have an opportunity to show you our homes. Sincerely yours, [113]

554 Dear Mr. Day: We realize that nobody likes to move before the Christmas holidays. But we can make it[1] worth your while.

Here at the new Grace Apartments we are about 85 percent rented and wish to close our renting[2] office. Therefore, in order to fill the remaining 15 percent, we will give each tenant moving in before[3] December 20 one month's occupancy free.

Residents of Grace Apartments enjoy many advantages,[4] including year-round air conditioning, a 24-hour guard, and low rent.

If you have been thinking of moving,[5] now is the time to do it. Stop in at our renting office and let one of our representatives show you[6] the fine apartments that are available. Select the one you like, move in before December 20, and save[7] a month's rent. Sincerely yours, [145]

555 Dear Mr. Davis: Our business is taking the tension out of relocating when a man is transferred from one[1] city to another. We help him select the right community and home in or near the city to which he[2] has been transferred.

When we find the home we think best suits a man's needs, we arrange for him to inspect it. If he decides[3] it is the one he wants, we move him.

Wouldn't you like this type of service when you must move? We are ready to[4] serve you. Sincerely yours, [84]

556   Dear Mr. West: I learned from my real estate agent that your home in Charleston will soon be for sale. I am[1] opening° a furniture store in Charleston in the near future, and I am interested in buying a home there.[2]

As we have three children of school age, the location of the home we choose is necessarily of great importance.[3] I would appreciate it if you would send me information concerning† schools and shopping centers near your[4] property. This information will be exceedingly helpful to me in determining whether I should make[5] a special visit to Charleston to see your house.

I hope to hear from you soon, Mr. West. Cordially yours,   [118]
Also correct:
°starting
†about, regarding

LESSON 65

559   *Buying a Home*

The best method of selecting a new home is to familiarize yourself with all the homes that are on the market.[1] This, of course, can be a big job, but you can simplify it considerably if you go to a reputable[2] real estate agent.

In large cities, real estate dealers offer many conveniences, one of[3] which is multiple listing. Multiple listing makes hundreds of homes that are on the market available to[4] you through a single agent.

Some dealers have television tapes made of the homes, and you are able to take a "tour" of[5] the house without actually going to the site. Many offices are open during the evening[6] hours. This makes selecting a house much easier if you work during the day.

Don't rush into making a choice too[7] quickly. You should probably take several weeks before you make a decision. The "bargain" all too often will[8] turn out not to be such a bargain after all if you give yourself plenty of time to consider it.

Before[9] you look at the first house, decide exactly what you must have. You will need to decide how many bedrooms are essential,[10] how many bathrooms are necessary, and what location is desirable. It is all too easy[11] to buy "more house" than you actually need when you see an attractive home in a nice neighborhood.

When you look[12] at the house, check to see if there are sufficient closets and ample storage facilities. Find out if there is[13] a garage. Determine if the land surrounding the house is suitable for your needs.

It is extremely important[14] that you look carefully at the floor plan of the house. Are the rooms located conveniently? Does the kitchen[15] provide a convenient work area? Will you have to take many needless steps in walking around the house because[16] of poorly located closets?

When you have looked at a number of homes, you should narrow your choice down to three or[17] four by examining each critically and ruling out those that do not meet your specifications.

Chances[18] are that you will not find a home that has every feature you would like. But with careful planning, you will find one[19] that will meet most of your needs. [385]

560 *Selling a Home*

Most people in America will one day be faced with the task of selling a home. This can be a very[1] difficult job, or it can be a relatively easy one. There are a number of "ground rules" that you should follow[2] when you are faced with the problem of selling a house.

First, you will want to take enough time to get a top price. Second,[3] you will want to present your house in the best possible light. Third, you will want to be sure that all negotiations[4] are handled in accordance with local and state laws.

You can simplify your job greatly if you will enter[5] into a contract for a specified period of time with a reputable real estate agent. Allow[6] yourself at least three months to sell your home.

Before you set a price on it, investigate the local market[7] to see what comparable homes are worth. Then set a reasonable, but competitive, price on your home.

Before[8] anyone takes a look at your house, be sure that it is in top-notch condition so that it creates a good initial[9] impression. A few dollars invested in paint may make a great deal of difference in the selling price.[10] No one likes to look at a house with old, cracked paint or at walls that are marked with dirt or fingerprints. Remember that[11] house hunters will also want to look at your closets, your garage, and even your attic.

If you have a yard, be[12] sure that it is neat and clean. Your grass should be freshly cut, and your shrubs should be trimmed.

If you are dealing with a real[13] estate agent, you will probably have all the legal help you need. However, you should be sure that every[14] legal step is taken before you sign final contracts. A call to your attorney could save you time and expense.[15]

The principal consideration in selling a home is to give yourself plenty of time. If you will do[16] this, you will probably find just the right buyer for your home. [331]

561 Dear Mr. Jennings: It doesn't make sense to move away from grandchildren when you retire. They are so much fun to[1] be with and to play with.

That is why so many retired people are moving to Leisure Village, which is only[2] 30 miles from New York.

At Leisure Village you can do as much or as little as you please. You can swim, play golf,[3] or go fishing. Or you can simply relax in pleasant surroundings.

So plan to retire in Leisure Village. Enjoy[4] the greatest retirement benefit of all—a new world of freedom without severing your ties with your family[5] and dear friends.

A booklet containing a description of Leisure Village and giving the cost of the units[6] that are available is enclosed. Call us if you have any questions. Better still, come and visit us. Sincerely[7] yours, [142]

Chapter 14

LESSON 66

564 Dear Mr. Overmeyer: Suitcases are very much like people; they cannot get by on looks alone. So when[1] Parker manufactures a fine suitcase, the result is more than just an ordinary good-looking travel bag.[2]

We make it strong by giving it a steel frame. We put a lock on it that will not open should the suitcase be dropped[3] accidentally. When we complete our work, our suitcase has another important quality—its beauty is[4] more than skin deep.

You will find traveling for business or pleasure a great deal more enjoyable when you carry[5] your things in Parker luggage.

The next time you need luggage of any kind, visit our nearest store. All our stores are listed[6] on the enclosed circular. Yours very truly,   [130]

565 Dear Mr. Casey: You were right and we were wrong!

You did write us a letter on July 1 in which you enclosed[1] a check for $300 and explained that you would pay the remaining $200 by August 15.[2] Through an error in our office, your payment was credited to the wrong account. We are sorry and promise to[3] try to avoid such a mistake again.

We look forward to continuing our pleasant business relationship[4] for many years to come. Sincerely yours,   [87]

566 Dear Mrs. Phillips: Thank you for your letter of August 20.

We are, of course, glad to accept for credit[1] merchandise which is returned to us within a reasonable time and which can be returned to stock for sale.

According[2] to our records, you purchased your suit more than two months ago. Under the circumstances, we regret that we[3] cannot accept it and are returning it to you by parcel post.

When you are in Westport, we hope you will come[4] in to see our new fashion collection. Yours truly,   [90]

567 Dear Mr. Lee: Because many years have gone by since Tom Sawyer enlisted the help of his friends to whitewash Aunt[1] Polly's fence in Hannibal, you may be surprised to learn that that fence is still standing. In recent years, however,[2] it has been necessary to use something more effective than whitewash to preserve the famous Tom Sawyer fence.[3] Some of its posts and planks had begun to rot.

Our organization, the Wilson Paint Company, was called in to[4] help. Our chemical division, which is constantly engaged in developing new, longer-lasting paints, applied[5] one of our special paints to the fence. Now the fence is safe from rot and deterioration for years to come.

If[6] you would like to have more information about Wilson interior and exterior paints, return the enclosed[7] card, and we will send you one of our colorful brochures describing all our products. Sincerely yours,   [157]

568 Dear Mr. Ross: It may take time, patience, and even a certain amount of tactful salesmanship to get a man[1] to try his first pair of Webber shoes. We do not worry, however, about his second pair. We know he will be[2] back. Once a man has experienced the wonderful comfort of Webber shoes, he is one of our fans forever.[3]

We hope that you will try your first pair soon. After you have worn the shoes for a while, you will wish that you had tried a[4] pair years ago.

Our prices range from $25 to $40, no more than you would have to pay for[5] any other fine shoes. Don't deprive yourself of the comfort and enjoyment of that first pair of Webber shoes. Come[6] in today. Cordially yours, [124]

569 Dear Mr. Hill: At its meeting on Friday, June 10, the board of directors of the Retail Business Association[1] voted to establish an annual scholarship award to be given to the outstanding senior[2] in distributive education at Milford High School. A special committee will administer the program[3] according to the following guidelines:

1. The recipient must be a senior studying distributive[4] education.
2. The faculty in distributive education will *nominate** three students for the award.[5]
3. After interviewing the three students, the special committee will select the winner.
4. The amount[6] of the award will be $500, and it may be used by the recipient to pay for tuition[7] in any college in the state.

I know, Mr. Hill, that as coordinator of distributive education[8] at Milford High School, you will be pleased with the establishment of this scholarship award. Sincerely yours,[9] [180]
Also correct:
*name, select

Office-Style Dictation

570 (*As dictated*) Dear Mr. Brown: One of the most difficult tasks [no, *unpleasant tasks*] that a businessman must face is announcing an increase in prices. However, because of the increase in the cost of labor and materials [add the world *large* before *increase*], we have no alternative but to increase our prices if we are to remain in business. [No, *continue in business.*] Therefore, beginning on July 15, the prices of all our lumber products will be increased 5 percent.

I am sure you will agree that this increase is a modest one. [Add *Mr. Brown* after *agree.*]

I sincerely hope that no further increase in our prices will be necessary in the immediate future. Yours very truly, [Scratch out the last sentence.]

570 (*As it would be transcribed*) Dear Mr. Brown: One of the most unpleasant tasks that a businessman must face is announcing an increase in prices.[1] However, because of the large increase in the cost of labor and materials, we have no alternative[2] but to increase our prices if we are to continue in business. Therefore, beginning on July 15,[3] the prices of all our lumber products will be increased 5 percent.

I am sure you will agree, Mr.

Brown, that[4] this increase is a modest one. Yours very truly, [89]

LESSON 67

575 Dear Mrs. Rich: Is your home crowded? If it is, you will be interested in our "space program" for crowded homes.[1]

The American washer is one of the most compact units ever manufactured. When it is not working,[2] it gets out of the way. It hides in a closet or rolls anywhere that is convenient.

Because the American[3] washer is on wheels, it is easily portable. To do a week's wash, all you have to do is put your laundry[4] into the washer, roll the washer up to a sink, hook it to the faucet, plug it into an electrical[5] outlet, and turn on a switch. In a few minutes your wash will be done. It is as simple as that.

We hope you[6] will visit us soon and let us show you the American washer. You will be fascinated with what you see.[7] Sincerely yours, [142]

576 Dear Mr. Taylor: You will be interested to know that you were the subject of a recent discussion between[1] our president and our credit manager. It started when the credit manager informed the president[2] that you had not used your charge account in several months. Naturally, things like this get our credit manager[3] and our president excited.

In order to calm everybody's nerves (and, incidentally, to make sure[4] that we continue offering you the best service), we are writing to ask why you have not been using your charge[5] account at our department store.

Have we done something that dissatisfied you? If we have, we certainly want to[6] know about it. We are always eager to provide the best possible service. If we displeased you as a result[7] of some human failing, we want to make amends.

Won't you stop in soon or drop us a few lines of explanation.[8] We would certainly appreciate it, Mr. Taylor. Sincerely yours, [173]

577 Dear Mr. Stevens: Welcome to our family of charge customers at the Greenville Department Store.

We invite[1] you to spend some time browsing through our store; come at any time to "just look around." But when you need help, you will find[2] our experienced, well-trained people ready and eager to wait on you.

We look forward to seeing you often.[3] Sincerely yours, [62]

578 Dear Mr. Stein: It is never a pleasant task for a merchant to have to announce an increase in prices. However,[1] we have no alternative but to raise prices if we are to remain in business. The cost of materials,[2] labor, and general overhead has risen so sharply during the past eight months that we can no longer[3] absorb it. The purpose of this letter, therefore, is to announce that on July 15 we will raise our prices[4] on custom-made suits 15 percent.

We are writing you and our other charge customers well in advance of[5] the date that the increase will take place so that you will have ample time to arrange to buy your winter wardrobe at[6] our present low prices. If you wish, you may select the things you want now and be billed for them on October 15.[7] Very truly yours, [143]

579 Dear Mr. Dale: We are pleased that you accepted our offer to send one of our representatives to your store[1] to demonstrate our new electric frying pans. Our past experience with this type of demonstration shows that[2] sales have increased over 200 percent during the two months following one of our demonstrations.

The date you[3] suggested, May 17, is a good time for us. We recommend, therefore, that you go ahead with your advertising[4] in the newspapers for that day.

Mr. Bradley Beck, our demonstrator, will be in your store from 9 a.m.[5] to 5 p.m. on Friday, May 17. Sincerely yours, [111]

580 Dear Mrs. O'Brien: The dress you returned by parcel post was received by our adjustment department this morning.[1] We are *happy** to exchange it for a size 12 in the same color and style. You should receive the new dress in about[2] ten days.

On May 15 the Nashville Department Store will be 60 years old. To celebrate this *occasion,*† we[3] will hold a fashion show each evening at 7 o'clock during the week of May 15. At this show we[4] propose to demonstrate the evolution of today's styles from those in vogue when we first opened our doors.

We will[5] also take a look at the present creations of outstanding con-temporary dress designers of both the[6] United States and other countries.

Don't miss this unique style show —you will enjoy every minute of it, Mrs.[7] O'Brien. Very truly yours, [145]

Also correct:
* glad
† event

LESSON 68

584 Dear Mrs. Buck: It is a pleasure for Simms and Company to invite you to a private sale of spring fashions[1] on Wednesday, April 9, on our seventh floor.

This special notice is being sent to you in advance of our[2] announcement to the general public so that you will have the first selection at important savings. You will find[3] suits, coats, and evening dresses at one-half their original prices.

This private sale will begin at 9[4] a.m. Our alert, well-trained staff will be ready to serve you. Sincerely yours, [93]

585 Dear Mrs. West: As you may know, Jennings and Company has operated a complete men's store since 1930.[1] However, many women who want quality suits and dresses have asked us to add a ladies' wear department.[2]

It is a pleasure to announce that on Friday, July 10, we will open such a department. We will offer[3] the women of Springfield the same style, precision fit, and expert workmanship that have made our men's store the place[4] where successful men prefer to shop.

We believe that you and your friends will want to visit this new and completely[5] modern department in the near future. We assure you that you will find shopping there an interesting, delightful[6] adventure. Yours very truly, [127]

586 Dear Mr. Thomas: If you were to buy a clock radio for music, you would be buying it for the wrong reason[1] because it is the clock, not the music, that has to get you up in the morning.

At Franklin's we have spent[2] 75 years making clocks that work perfectly. Now we are putting clocks into radios.

For the first time you[3] can purchase a clock with more than just a radio in mind. That does not mean that you have to give up radio[4] quality to get clock quality. We apply the same standards to our radios that we apply to our clocks.[5]

Our clock radios are more than just functional; they are beautifully designed appliances.

Enclosed is an[6] insert that shows the different styles of clock radios that are available from your Franklin dealer. Sincerely[7] yours, [142]

587 Dear Mrs. Camp: Welcome to Ashland. May we extend a cordial invitation to you to make Nash's Department[1] Store your shopping headquarters.

For the convenience of shoppers, Nash's has three locations: the main store on Broad[2] Street, the Shore Road store, and the East Side store.

All three have fine lunchrooms in which you can enjoy a leisurely meal or[3] snack after your shopping is finished.

When your time is limited, you can take advantage of our mail and telephone[4] order services and do your shopping directly from your own home. If you would like to open a charge account,[5] the enclosed brochure will show you how easy it is to do so.

At Nash's we exert ourselves to please you.[6] We hope to see you soon. Sincerely yours, [127]

588 Dear Mr. Weeks: During the past several weeks we have tried to make Christmas shopping more convenient for our[1] customers by keeping our store open until 9 p.m. on weekdays. Many people have told us that it was a[2] great convenience to them and that they wished we would remain open until 9 p.m. throughout the year.

Consequently,[3] we have decided to give the idea a trial. During January and February we will remain[4] open every weekday until 9 p.m. We will continue to remain open until 6 p.m.[5] on Saturdays.

We invite you to take advantage of these late shopping hours the next time you need anything from[6] our store. Cordially yours, [124]

589 Gentlemen: We were sorry to learn that our last shipment of lamps arrived in damaged condition. Please hold the shipment[1] for inspection by our local representative, Mr. James Smith. He will call on you sometime during the[2] week of December 7 to determine who is responsible for the damage.

In the meantime, we are sending[3] you a duplicate shipment, which should arrive in about three days. We regret any inconvenience you have been[4] caused. Yours truly, [83]

590 Dear Mr. Green: Can you enter a store merely to browse without feeling a bit self-conscious when a clerk asks you[1] whether he can help you? Some men, unfortunately, are terrified at the *thought** of going into a men's shop[2] without buying anything. This is a pity.

The well-read man is usually the man who makes a habit[3] of looking through bookstores. The man who "looks like a million" in the clothes he wears is the one who knows what is being[4] shown in the better stores and who takes time deciding what he wants to wear. The man who rushes in, buys something, and[5] rushes out is cheating himself. He may *buy†* good clothes, but he is not likely to look his best in them.

Why not come[6] in soon to the Smith Clothing Store and just browse around. If you find something you like, one of our salesmen will be glad[7] to wait on you. If you don't and leave without buying anything, we will understand. Cordially yours, [158]

Also correct:
*idea
†purchase, obtain

LESSON 69

594 Dear Mr. Pierce: Thank you for writing us about the partial shipment of merchandise you ordered on May 1. We[1] understand your disappointment in not receiving the bedroom and living room suites at the same time you received[2] the other items. We have good news, however. Just this morning we had a telegram from the manufacturer[3] informing us that we may expect the furniture to arrive at our warehouse in a few days. Consequently,[4] we should be able to deliver it by the first of next week.

May we take this opportunity, Mr. Pierce,[5] to express to you our sincere appreciation for the business you have given us during the past ten years.[6] Sincerely yours, [122]

595 Dear Mr. Ramsey: Thank you for applying for an account with Jones and Company. We are happy that you enjoy[1] shopping in the friendly atmosphere of our store, and we hope you will visit us frequently in the future.[2] We regret, however, that we are unable to grant you a credit card at this time for the following reasons:[3]

1. You have lived in Wilmington for only a short time and have not yet obtained permanent employment here.[4]

2. You are not able to provide us with any credit references in Washington, where you lived during[5] the past five years.

When you have lived in Wilmington for six months and have obtained permanent employment here, we will[6] be glad to reconsider your application for credit.

In the meantime, Mr. Ramsey, we will be delighted[7] to serve you as a cash customer. We look forward to seeing you soon. Cordially yours, [157]

596 Dear Mr. Stephens: Several months ago I moved from Huntington to Hartford. Before I left, I visited[1] your accounting department and asked one of your clerks to close out my account. The clerk assured me that this would be[2] done promptly.

Today I received a statement which had been forwarded to my home in Hartford. On the statement were[3] six items charged to my account two weeks after I had moved away from Huntington.

I would appreciate your[4] checking into this matter to find out whether you have made a mistake or whether someone is using my former[5] account illegally. Yours very truly, [109]

597 Dear Miss Curtiss: A special representative of the Lexington Cosmetics Company, Miss Julie Mason,[1] will be in our department store on Tuesday, Wednesday, and Thursday, September 6, 7, and 8, to discuss[2] the proper use of cosmetics with our customers.

Miss Mason, who is a well-known authority in the field,[3] will be glad to give you personal help in the selection of cosmetics that are exactly right for you. We[4] know that many people will want to consult Miss Mason; therefore, we suggest that you fill out and return the enclosed[5] card indicating a convenient time for you, and we will schedule a 20-minute appointment for you.[6]

There is, of course, no charge for this service. Sincerely yours, [130]

598 Dear Mr. Day: At the Baker Furniture Store we stand behind every piece of furniture that we sell. It[1] doesn't make any difference whether you buy a $40 lamp or a $400 sofa; we[2] make sure that every piece we sell you arrives in your home in perfect condition.

When the furniture is delivered[3] to your home, we examine it for nicks and scratches and make whatever adjustments are necessary.[4] Even if a problem develops afterwards, we do everything possible to make you happy.

Come in[5] when you need furniture for your home. You will find plenty of free parking space. We are open from 10 a.m. to[6] 9 p.m. Mondays through Fridays; from 9 a.m. to 6 p.m on Saturdays. Sincerely yours, [137]

599 Dear Mrs. Green: We are moving. After serving the citizens of Westport for more than 20 years at 111[1] Park Road, the Westport Flower Shop will move on July 1 to 316 West Street, which is opposite the[2] post office. We are moving to these new quarters because we have outgrown our present ones. In our new quarters we will[3] be able to carry a larger variety of plants and flowers and be able to serve your flower needs[4] more efficiently.

We are looking forward to seeing you at our grand opening on Monday, July 1. Very[5] truly yours, [102]

600 Dear Mr. Day: As you know,

your account is now more than eight weeks past due. We have written you four letters requesting[1] payment, but we have not had so much as an acknowledgment from you. The time has come when we must take definite[2] steps to collect the $600 you owe us.

If we do not receive a *check**** from you by July 30,[3] we will turn your account over to our attorney for collection. You realize, of course, that our taking[4] this action will greatly weaken your credit standing.

Please don't force us to do this; send us your check today. Yours very[5] truly, [101]
Also correct:
***payment, remittance

LESSON 70

603 *Changes in Retailing*

One of America's most dynamic and basic industries is in a state of change. Retailing, the very[1] symbol of American free enterprise, has gone through many stages of development, and the evolution[2] continues today.

America's retailing, which started with bartering only a few hundred years ago,[3] has progressed to the full-line department stores and specialty shops of today. In recent years, however, many[4] retail stores have moved to the suburbs or have opened branches in the suburbs as American families[5] moved away from the central cities. When the buying public changed residence, the retail stores followed. Thus, vast shopping[6] centers and plazas have opened in the middle of residential areas, bring-

ing retail business to[7] the public.

This change in retail location has, to a great extent, been dependent upon the automobile,[8] which allowed great mobility of the population. But definite and worthwhile changes are still occurring.[9] The number of automobiles has increased so greatly that congestion and pollution are major problems[10] in both large and small cities. Consequently, a new direction in retailing may be indicated.

Some major[11] stores now offer a 24-hour telephone ordering service, "shopping in your home" service, and a return[12] to catalog sales.

In the future, goods may be advertised on cable television, and orders may be[13] placed either through the television set itself or by telephone.

Retailing, the symbol of free enterprise,[14] has changed and will continue to change to meet the new demands and desires of the buying public. [297]

604 *The Discount Store*

One of the most interesting innovations in retailing during the past few years has been the development[1] of the discount department store. Actually, a discount house is nothing more than a "price-appeal" department[2] store.

The main differences between discount stores and regular department stores lie in the following areas:[3]

1. The location and decoration of the building.

2. The sales personnel.

3. The size and packaging[4] of merchandise.

The building is usually located in an area surrounded by a large parking[5] lot and near a major highway. It is not always located in a shopping center; however, it is[6] usually within a few blocks of one. The interior of the building is sometimes unfinished, giving[7] the appearance of frugality.

The sales personnel are usually stationed behind check-out counters, and[8] special help in shopping is available only if the customer requests it.

Often in discount stores, goods[9] are sold in large volume, and in many of these stores it may be impossible to buy in small quantities. Large[10] items are often prepackaged. The customer first makes a selection and pays for it. Then the prepackaged item[11] is delivered to the front of the store, where the customer picks it up.

The success of the "price-appeal" department[12] store has been phenomenal in recent years, and indications are that this type of retail store will[13] continue to be popular. [264]

605 Gentlemen: The set of glasses that I purchased at your store on June 18 was delivered today. When I opened[1] the package, I found that three of the glasses were broken. Apparently they were not packed carefully enough[2] to prevent breakage in transit. I am returning the entire shipment so that you can see the condition in[3] which it arrived.

I would appreciate your sending me another set so that it reaches me by July 15.[4] Cordially yours, [83]

606 Dear Mr. James: Enclosed is our new catalog. We are mailing it to you in October so that you will have[1] plenty of time in which to choose the presents you wish to give to your friends and to your family.

This new catalog[2] has hundreds of new and original gift ideas for men and women as well as for children of all[3] ages.

Simply sit back in your easy chair, look through the catalog, and list your selections on the handy order[4] blank in the back of the catalog. When you are finished, add up the cost of your selections, attach your check,[5] and mail everything to us in the envelope that is also enclosed. We will do the rest.

Isn't that an easy[6] way to do your Christmas shopping? Very truly yours, [130]

607 Dear Mrs. Barnes: Thank you for your order for our No. 1181 grill. This is a very popular model[1] with people who like to cook outdoors.

Unfortunately, we cannot ship this grill to you directly as we[2] are wholesalers and sell only to authorized dealers.

Our dealer in Salem is the National Appliance[3] Company, which is located at 416 West Street. We are sure that they will be delighted to show you their[4] complete line of grills as well as the other appliances that we manufacture.

Why not visit them today.[5] Sincerely yours, [102]

608 Dear Mrs. Kelly: It is a pleasure to welcome you as a new credit account customer at the National[1] Department Stores. Your charge plate is enclosed; we hope that you will have many opportunities to use it. Your[2] plate will be honored at all our stores in New York, Yonkers, and White Plains. Please take a moment now to sign the card.

If[3] at anytime you have suggestions on how we can improve our service or our merchandise, please be sure to let[4] us know. Sincerely yours, [84]

Chapter 15

LESSON 71

611 Dear Miss James: As a service to the schools of America, the public relations department of the National[1] Railroad has prepared a short film that depicts the important part that the railroads have played during the last hundred[2] years in the development of our country. Any school wishing to show this film to its student body need only[3] request us to send it to them.

If you would like to show this film in your school, simply fill out the enclosed[4] form and return it to us in the envelope that is also enclosed. On the form indicate several[5] alternative dates on which you would be able to show the film. Yours very truly, [114]

612 Dear Mr. Sullivan: Hartford College is exploring the possibility of sponsoring a European[1] tour this summer for interested students.

We would like to make arrangements with a well-known company such[2] as yours to handle the details. Our college would organize the group and arrange for staff members to serve as[3] counselors. We hope to offer the tour as an annual course in which a student may enroll for college credit.[4]

Will you please send us information about your tours and the accommodations and services that you could provide.[5]

Since we are eager to complete our plans as soon as possible, we would appreciate hearing from you soon.[6] Yours very truly, [123]

613 Dear Mr. Baxter: When you have to send a package in a hurry, send it by Imperial Bus Lines. We can[1] handle any package that weighs 100 pounds or less. Our service is not only fast but also economical.[2]

Imperial Bus Lines can take packages anywhere they take people, and that is almost everywhere.[3] Because Imperial buses travel day and night seven days a week, your package will not be shelved over[4] a weekend or a holiday. Most buses arrive at their destination within 24 hours.

If you have[5] something special to send, call Imperial Bus Lines; then, Mr. Baxter, leave the rest to us. Sincerely yours,[6] [120]

614 To the Staff: On Monday, May 21, the First Avenue entrance to the subway located in our building[1] will be closed for remodeling and repairs. The Transit Authority estimates that this entrance will remain[2] closed approximately six months. During this time the station will be enlarged, an escalator will be installed,[3] and new tile flooring will be laid.

We are sorry that it will be necessary for the Transit Authority[4] to close this entrance temporarily, but the improvements will make both the subway and our building more attractive[5] and convenient. C. R. Stone [105]

615 Dear Mr. Day: More and more businessmen are planning their own flight itineraries to make sure that they travel[1] the best way and cover the most ground. They are planning them with the help of the *Airline Guide*. Why not follow their[2] example.

To use the *Airline Guide*, you simply look up your destination city. Under that listing, you locate[3] your departure city, and there you will find all the facts you need to plan your flight.

For a trial subscription to[4] the *Airline Guide*, complete and return the enclosed card. Upon its receipt, we will send you an *Airline Guide* to use[5] for ten days. If after that time you do not agree that it provides a helpful service, just return our invoice[6] marked "Cancel" and you owe us nothing. Sincerely yours, [130]

616 Dear Mr. Green: Thank you for writing us about the film your organization has developed showing the many[1] contributions the railroads have made in the development of our country.

The *children** in our school take up[2] the railroad industry in the sixth grade, which is taught by Mrs. Alice C. Smith. Mrs. Smith is very much[3] interested in showing the film to her class. The best time for her would be November 14, 15, or 16.[4]

If you could send us the film for showing on one of these days, we would be grateful, Mr. Green. Sincerely yours,[5] [100]

Also correct:
*students

Office-Style Dictation

617 (*As dictated*) Dear Mr. Smith: In a few days our new booklet entitled *What College Men Are Wearing* will be off the press. This booklet shows [no, *describes;* oh, leave it *shows*] what clothes are preferred at the various colleges in the country. The material in the booklet was compiled [change that to *organized;* on second thought, perhaps *compiled* would be better] on the basis of several thousand answers we received to a questionnaire we sent [no, *mailed;* no, *sent*] to college presidents, deans, and others who were in a position to advise us. A complimentary copy of this booklet [*useful booklet*] is yours for the asking. You can pick it up at one of our stores. If it is more convenient to telephone us or mail us a card requesting [no, *asking for;* oh, leave *requesting*] a copy you may do so. One will be sent to you immediately. [Scratch out that last sentence.]

After you have studied the booklet, come in and select the things you will need for college next fall, Sincerely yours, [Change *things* to *clothes*.]

617 (*As it would be transcribed*) Dear Mr. Smith: In a few days our new booklet entitled *What College Men Are Wearing* will be off the press. This[1] booklet shows what clothes are preferred at the various colleges in the country. The material in the booklet[2] was compiled on the basis of several thousand answers we received to a questionnaire we sent to college[3] presidents, deans, and others who were in a position to advise us. A complimentary copy of this[4] useful booklet is yours for the asking. You can pick it up at one of our stores. If it is more convenient[5] to telephone us or mail us a card requesting a copy, you may do so.

After you have studied the booklet,[6] come in and select the clothes you will need for college next fall. Sincerely yours, [133]

LESSON 72

622 Mr. Davis: As you will recall, one of the most important problems we discussed in our meeting several[1] days ago was the lack of working capital. Perhaps we could solve this problem by selling our trucks and leasing[2] whatever trucks we may need in the future. The sale of our present fleet would have the effect of making available[3] to us more than $300,000 of badly needed capital.

When Mr. Green and I[4] were in Chicago on Friday, June 16, we talked to representatives of five of the major leasing[5] organizations. In our opinion, the Stevens Company

offers one of the best plans.

I suggest that we invite[6] the Stevens Company to submit a leasing proposal to us as soon as possible. J. C. James [138]

623 Mr. James: Your suggestion that we investigate the possibility of leasing trucks in the future is[1] one that we must consider seriously. As you know, the problem of obtaining working capital has become[2] even more acute during the past few months, and we must do something about it soon.

Would you be good enough to[3] get three or four bids from buyers of used trucks and to ask the Stevens Company to submit a leasing proposal[4] to us as soon as possible.

When you have gathered this information, please prepare a report on how you[5] feel our switch to leasing will affect the company's financial picture in the future. As soon as I receive[6] this report, I will call a special meeting of the finance committee to consider the whole matter of leasing.[7] Harry Davis [142]

624 Gentlemen: For several months the Greenburg Merchants Association has been looking for ways to increase business[1] in the uptown area. We are now considering the possibility of offering free transportation[2] on city buses to shoppers between the hours of 10 a.m. and 3 p.m. Monday through Friday.

Since[3] you have such a plan currently in operation in Harrisburg, we would appreciate your telling us what[4] effect it has had on retail sales.

If you know of any other cities where this arrangement has been used[5] successfully during the past year, we would appreciate your sending us that information as well.

Thank you for[6] your help. Very truly yours, [125]

625 Dear Mr. Milton: You will remember that on November 20 you wrote us that one of the tables that we[1] shipped you on November 15 arrived in damaged condition; in fact, it was a total loss and could not be[2] repaired.

As soon as we received your letter, we notified the Pittsburgh Trucking Company, which delivered the[3] tables to you. We have just received a letter from them telling us that in order to settle this claim, they need[4] the information requested on the enclosed form. Will you please fill out the form and mail it to them as soon as[5] possible.

In the meantime, Mr. Milton, we have sent you another table exactly like the one that was[6] damaged. We hope that you have not been seriously inconvenienced as a result of this incident. Very[7] truly yours, [142]

626 Dear Mr. Walker: We regret that our train from New York to Chicago no longer stops at Weston. We understand[1] the disappointment you expressed in your letter of June 18.

As you probably know, Amtrak train service[2] is now in effect. As a result, most train schedules have been changed completely.

Passenger train service in the[3] nation has been under great economic strain during recent years, and Amtrak is attempting to revitalize[4] this service through reduced schedules on little-used routes and improved service on the more frequently used lines.

We[5] are sorry for the inconvenience the change in schedule has caused you, but we hope that in the future we will be[6] able to serve your needs and the needs of the entire country in a much better way. Sincerely yours, [138]

627 Dear Mr. Burns: As you will recall, last year you were kind enough to have one of your buses make a special stop[1] at Parkersburg so that I could board it at that point. Since June 2, however, circumstances have made it unnecessary[2] for me to take this bus. Beginning August 4, I would like once again to board the bus at Parkersburg[3] each morning Monday through Friday. Will you please let me know *whether** you can arrange this for me.

My return trip from[4] Pittsburgh to Parkersburg presents no problem. I will take the regularly scheduled 5 o'clock bus.

I sincerely[5] appreciate the thoughtful, courteous service that your *organization†* has provided me in the past.[6] Sincerely yours, [122]
Also correct:
**if
†company, bus line

LESSON 73

631 Dear Mr. Mason: As you know, your company has had our trucking business for many years, and in general[1] we have been well satisfied with your service. We regret to tell you, however, that in recent months your service[2] has deteriorated. Our warehousemen tell us that some of your trucks have been dirty and others contained debris[3] left over from previous shipments. As a result, our merchandise has been arriving at our branches in[4] unsatisfactory condition.

Please give this matter your prompt, careful attention. As you are aware, we give[5] your company a substantial amount of business each year. It is our desire to continue dealing with you,[6] but we will not be able to do so if the conditions I have described are not immediately corrected.[7] Very truly yours, [143]

632 Dear Mr. Bright: Enclosed is my check for $200 to cover the cost of your services in moving[1] our furniture to our new home on Tuesday, July 18.

I appreciate the efficiency and thoughtfulness[2] of your men in moving our furniture. My family and I were out of town at the time of the move. When[3] we entered our new house upon our return and saw that the furniture had been placed in the rooms exactly as[4] we had requested, we were delighted.

You can see that we are sold on the Smith Moving Company's efficiency.[5] You may be sure that any time we have an opportunity to recommend your company, we will[6] certainly do so. Sincerely yours, [126]

633 Dear Stockholder: The annual meeting of the stockholders of the Ohio Central Railroad will be held on[1] Wednesday, March 15, at 10 a.m. in Room 2011 of the Blair Hotel.

The agenda for this meeting[2] is as follows:

1. Election of three new directors for three-year terms.

2. Consideration of a slight increase[3] in transportation rates.

3. Study of regulations governing passenger and freight service to our customers.[4]

4. Presentation of the annual report.

We hope you will be able to attend this meeting. If[5] you are unable to do so, please sign and return the enclosed proxy statement. Sincerely yours, [117]

634 Gentlemen: Our organization has decided to lease cars for our 50 salesmen for the coming year. We[1] understand that by leasing cars instead of buying them, we will be able to make substantial savings and at[2] the same time realize working capital for other projects.

Attached is a list of the special items we[3] would want installed in the cars that we lease. Please include the installation of these items in any bid that you[4] submit. Sincerely yours, [83]

635 Dear Mr. Peters: Enclosed is our bid covering the leasing of 50 Chargers for the coming year. As you[1] specified in your letter of January 20, we have included in our bid the installation of seven[2] special items.

Our company offers several advantages that other organizations cannot[3] match. As you consider our bid, please keep the following facts in mind:

1. Our cars are delivered to you in[4] top-notch condition. We test-drive the cars for 100 miles before delivery.

2. Our service departments, which[5] are located in all major cities, are open 24 hours a day. If one of your salesmen should have a[6] problem with his car at any time of the day or night, all he has to do is call the nearest one. Our well-trained mechanics[7] will service his car promptly.

3. We give overnight service on many types of repairs.

4. If one[8] of your salesmen should be stranded on the road because of engine trouble, we will deliver a replacement car[9] to him.

If there are any questions I can answer for you about our leasing plan, please call me at[10] 161-5551, Extension 1161. Sincerely yours, [210]

636 Dear Mr. Gates: We are disturbed by your complaint about the poor condition of the trucks in which your merchandise[1] has been delivered to your branches. We assure you, Mr. Gates, that we will investigate this situation[2] promptly.

In order to solve this problem, we will need your cooperation. Please *ask°* your employees to keep[3] accurate, detailed reports regarding the condition of our trucks and send these reports to us at the end of the month.[4]

After we have studied these reports carefully, we will be able to make any adjustments that are necessary.[5] Sincerely yours, [103]
Also correct:
°request, instruct

LESSON 74

640 Dear Mr. Wallace: No doubt in an organization like yours, with branch offices in many states, you occasionally[1] find it necessary to transfer a man from one area of the country to another. As[2] I am sure you have learned from experience, this can be very expensive. The company must, of course, pay the[3] costs of moving the employee and his family. It is also often necessary to finance several[4] trips by the employee to his new location before he can find suitable housing.

Carlson Van Lines has[5] established a new service that can help companies like yours to keep employee moving costs at a minimum—the[6] Carlson house-locating service.

This service can provide you with a listing of the available housing[7] for rent or for sale so that your employee will know what is available before he makes his first visit to[8] the new city.

When your employee has found the house he wants, we can then take over the complete job of moving[9] his furniture, clothing, and other personal property.

Please give us an opportunity to serve you the next[10] time you must transfer one of your employees. Sincerely yours, [211]

641 Gentlemen: The house-locating

service that your company offers appeals to us very much. As you point out,[1] it is expensive to send a man to a new location to find living quarters. An even more important[2] factor, however, is that the man must be away from his job at the very time that he is needed to complete[3] work that must be done before the transfer is made.

At the present time, one of our employees, Mr. J. M.[4] Brown, is being transferred from our home office to Albany. Mr. Brown is married and has three small children. The[5] Browns would like a house with four bedrooms that sells for no more than $40,000.

If you will send us information[6] on available houses in Albany that meet the above specifications, we will appreciate[7] it very much. Sincerely yours,   [145]

642 Dear Mr. Williams: In the course of a normal day's business, you no doubt find it necessary to send packages[1] from one office to another within the city. If you ask one of your regular employees to deliver[2] a package, he may have to be away from his office for several hours. The result is a loss[3] of valuable service and time. If you own a delivery truck, it probably sits idle most of the[4] time.

There is an alternative to this costly way to handle deliveries within the city: Use the services[5] of the Reliable Delivery Company.

Reliable is a new company specializing[6] in quick delivery of all types of packages from one office to another within the city. A[7] call to 112-

1122 will bring one of our dependable men to your office within minutes. He[8] will pick up your package and deliver it quickly. The cost is reasonable; the service is swift. Sincerely yours,[9]   [180]

643 Dear Mr. Easter: We recently read in the newspaper that your company has purchased a new building and[1] that you will be moving to your new quarters in February. Before that time, you will no doubt be facing many[2] problems in preparing to move. Why not let the Acme Moving Service take many of the worries of moving[3] off your mind.

Our company can arrange to pack everything in your old office and move it safely and[4] efficiently to the new location in the shortest possible time and at a cost which is surprisingly[5] low.

Why not let one of our well-trained representatives come to your office and discuss your move with you. Simply[6] indicate on the enclosed card when he may call and mail it. Sincerely yours,   [134]

644 Dear Passenger: Last week three passengers on our main line lost their lives while trying to save a few minutes and a[1] few steps. They tried to cross the tracks instead of using the bridges and overpasses provided at our stations.[2] These tragedies would not have happened if the victims had followed established regulations or common rules of[3] safety.

Railroads continue to be the safest means of transportation. However, a minority of passengers[4] persist in violating safety regulations before boarding trains and after leaving them. If this is[5] one of your temptations, please don't give in to it.

Your safety is our concern, but we need your help. The Central Railroad[6] [120]

645 Dear Mr. Ford: If you scratch a piece of furniture, you forget about it. However, we worry if a piece[1] of furniture is scratched when we move it. You see, it is our job to be as careful as possible when we move[2] your effects. When we scratch something, you have a right to complain.

That is why at Western Vans we spend more time and money[3] than other moving companies to train our people to think of your effects as fragile things. Consequently,[4] we don't pack a fine vase the same way that we pack pots and pans. In fact, we use 16 different *kinds*° of cartons[5] for packing different things. That is just one example of the meticulous attention you can expect from[6] Western Vans.

The next time you must move, *call*† us. We will move you quickly, efficiently, and inexpensively. Sincerely[7] yours, [141]
Also correct:
°types
†telephone, write

LESSON 75

648 *Revolution in Transportation*

Since the turn of the century, transportation in the United States has undergone rapid and dramatic[1] changes. It is interesting to note that only a few decades ago man was still dependent on horse-drawn[2] vehicles for transportation. Since that time, however, the automobile—the "horseless carriage"—has become[3] America's basic means of transportation. The automobile has probably created more changes in life style[4] in America than any other single invention. It has made it possible for people to live great[5] distances from their work and commute easily.

The train, which had a great role in the development of the western[6] United States, has undergone probably the most dramatic changes of any means of transportation.[7] For many years, trains were the favored means for long-distance travel. Since the invention of the airplane, however,[8] passenger service has been reduced to such an extent that few railroad lines now operate at a profit. However,[9] recent developments in high-speed commuter lines are encouraging interest in new railroads, particularly[10] in heavily populated areas.

The development of the air industry has been overwhelming.[11] Since the first flight at Kitty Hawk, the industry has grown from the hobby of two brothers into one of[12] the basic means of transportation in the world. Jumbo jets now carry hundreds of passengers in comfort over[13] vast distances at almost the speed of sound.

But with advantages come disadvantages. It is unfortunate,[14] but almost all major methods of transportation cause air pollution. And congestion has caused city[15] planners to look for new methods of transportation.

The first "people movers," long moving sidewalks designed to move[16] thousands of people from one part of town to another, are now in the experimental stage.

An immediate[17] step to alleviate congestion is in the redesign of cities themselves, thus altering the need for[18] standard types of transportation. Some buildings are now being constructed which contain apartments, schools, stores, and offices,[19] all in the same tower. For people who live and work in this type of building, the need to commute has already[20] been changed. In effect, the commuting in such buildings is done by elevator rather than by car![21] Vertical transportation may become far more important in the future than it has ever been before.

Man has[22] come to depend on transportation for mobility. The time may be close at hand, however, when he must[23] restructure his thinking and his life concerning his need to move about. Transportation is indeed in a state of[24] revolution.   [483]

649 Dear Passenger: As you know, this was the first morning we operated on our new zone schedules on the main line.[1] Please do not judge zone schedules by our first day's performance. While this is of no consequence to you, you should know that[2] this morning's difficulty was due to reasons totally unrelated to scheduling.

We have personnel[3] riding on each of the morning rush-hour trains to determine the number of passengers and the availability[4] of seats.

While we endeavored to assign the proper number of cars to provide a seat for every[5] commuter, we did miscalculate our needs for many trains. We are confident, however, that after several[6] days of normal operations, we will have a reliable basis for adjustments in train makeups.

The[7] comfort of our passengers is a matter of both professional and personal concern to us, and we are[8] doing everything possible to provide you with seats and reliable schedules. The Central Railroad[9]   [180]

650 Dear Mr. Barnes: The next time you must travel to Washington from New York, go by Eastern Bus Lines. You will enjoy[1] a comfortable, quick, and smooth trip and arrive in Washington refreshed.

We have recently put into service a[2] fleet of 60 new buses that are the last word in clean, modern comfort. These buses are air-conditioned and contain[3] rest rooms and reclining seats. We will get you to Washington for less money, too—only $16.

Our[4] buses leave the West Side Terminal every hour on the hour from 8 a.m. to 8 p.m. every day.[5]

So when you must go to Washington, go by Eastern Bus Lines. You do not need a reservation. Sincerely yours,[6]   [120]

651 Dear Mr. Banker: Have you often wished you could visit Denmark but felt your budget would not stand it? Well, here is[1] your opportunity to spend eight days in Copenhagen for only $305. This price includes[2] transportation, seven nights at a fine hotel, tickets to the Royal Danish Ballet, and many other items.³

If you would like complete details about this fine offer, fill out and return the enclosed card. Yours truly,⁴ [80]

652 Dear Passenger: The Christmas holidays will soon be here, and we are making plans for our special Christmas and New¹ Year's train schedules.

So that we may plan this service more effectively, we are asking you to complete the short survey² form that is attached. As you will see, the form asks you to try to determine your travel plans as they affect³ the Thursday and Friday preceding the Christmas and New Year's holidays.

Your cooperation in filling out⁴ this form will be of great assistance to us. When you have completed the form, hand it to the conductor. The Central⁵ Railroad [102]

Chapter 16

LESSON 76

655 Dear Mr. Worth: Thank you for the opportunity to assist you in planning your trip to the World Progress¹ Exposition in Great Falls in August.

We suggest that you take one of the two routes that are marked on the enclosed map.² The one marked in yellow is the shorter route; the one marked in blue is the more scenic route.

We are also enclosing³ a handy booklet that will answer any questions you may have regarding traffic regulations in the⁴ particular states through which you will be traveling.

If you are in doubt about which road to take on your trip, stop⁵ at one of our service stations. Our attendants will be glad to give you accurate directions.

Have a good time⁶ on your trip and please drive carefully. Sincerely yours, [130]

656 Mr. Sims: You will recall that on Friday, April 12, you asked me to reserve a seat for you on the Metroliner¹ from New York to Washington that leaves New York at 8 a.m. on July 4. This train has been completely² booked because of the heavy holiday travel. However, there is a regular train that leaves New York at 9³ a.m. Tickets are available for this train, but seats are not reserved. It will be necessary for you to⁴ arrive at the station early to get a good seat.

If you want me to purchase a ticket for you on the⁵ 9 a.m. train, please let me know. A. J. Green [107]

657 Dear Mr. Keller: We are happy to send you the information you requested about our European¹ tours.

We have two tours that include the Scandinavian countries: Sweden, Norway, and Denmark. One tour leaves New York² on June 5 and returns on June 30. This tour also includes visits to England and Scotland. The other[3] tour leaves on July 20 and includes the Scandinavian countries only.

The enclosed travel folders contain[4] detailed itineraries for both of these tours as well as a list of the types of accommodations[5] available and their cost.

Please feel free to write or call us for the answers to any further questions you may have.[6] We look forward, Mr. Keller, to the opportunity of helping you plan your trip to Europe. Yours very[7] truly, [141]

658 Dear Mr. Jones: If you are like many other people, you read the travel advertisements in newspapers and[1] magazines and then wistfully say to yourself, "That trip looks wonderful, but I can't possibly afford it." If[2] you own a Globe Mobile Home, however, all the travel adventure you have dreamed about can suddenly become[3] a reality.

A Globe Mobile Home brings the cost of travel down to fit the budget of the average family.[4] It saves you the bother of making complicated plans and reservations. You can travel at your own[5] speed with no regular schedule to follow. You can enjoy home cooking wherever you go; you do not have to[6] take your chances on "highway food."

We have all our models on display in our lot at 240 Main Street in Macon.[7] Why not come to see us soon and let us show them to you. Among these models you are sure to find one just right[8] for you and your family. Very truly yours, [169]

659 Dear Mr. Davis: If you have an urge to visit the Orient, let Japanese Airlines take you there.

From the[1] moment you board one of our planes, you will relax in an atmosphere that is decidedly Japanese. You will[2] be served either American or Japanese food by our friendly stewardesses.

When you arrive at your[3] destination, we can tell you what to see and where to buy. We will make your *trip** one that you will never forget.

To[4] make travel arrangements to the Orient, call us at 161-1222. Or if you prefer, see your[5] own travel agent. Yours very truly, [107]
Also correct:
*journey

Office-Style Dictation

660 (*As dictated*) Dear Mr. Jones: Our mutual friend, Mr. Charles C. Green, tells me that you are interested in planning a trip to Spain for yourself and your family [make that *for your family and yourself*] during the month of June. He asked me to offer you the services of my organization, the National Steamship Line. Needless to say, it will be a pleasure to do so.

Our travel experts will be delighted to help you in every way they can without, of course, any obligation on your part.

I am enclosing a booklet that describes and lists [no, *lists and describes*] our sailings to Spain and the accommodations that are available on the "Atlantic Queen" and the "President Jackson."

May I make this suggestion, Mr. Jones: If you decide to make this trip, make your bookings without delay. Travel to Spain is quite heavy in June. Sincerely yours,

660 (*As it would be transcribed*) Dear Mr. Jones: Our mutual friend, Mr. Charles C. Green, tells me that you are interested in planning a trip[1] to Spain for your family and yourself during the month of June. He asked me to offer you the services of[2] my organization, the National Steamship Line. Needless to say, it will be a pleasure to do so.

Our travel[3] experts will be delighted to help you in every way they can without, of course, any obligation on[4] your part.

I am enclosing a booklet that lists and describes our sailings to Spain and the accommodations that[5] are available on the "Atlantic Queen" and the "President Jackson."

May I make this suggestion, Mr. Jones:[6] If you decide to make this trip, make your bookings without delay. Travel to Spain is quite heavy in June. Sincerely[7] yours,   [141]

LESSON 77

665 Dear Mr. Bailey: All travel agencies sell their products—tickets— at the same price. The reason is, of course, that[1] they purchase their tickets from the same sources. Therefore, the difference between what you get from one travel agency[2] and another is not in price, Mr. Bailey, but in service.

The Cramer Travel Agency has been[3] providing that "something extra" in the way of service for many years. As a result, we are today one of the[4] most respected travel agencies in the world.

When you have Cramer arrange your travel, you receive service that[5] is prompt, courteous, and efficient.

Why not let us plan your next trip for you. Cordially yours,   [117]

666 Dear Mr. Patterson: One of the innovations in traveling is the trailer-trip excursion sponsored by[1] the National Trailer Association.

A trailer tour has many of the best features of a regular[2] guided tour. The itinerary is planned to include the most interesting places wherever you may be[3] traveling, and an experienced leader guides you and answers your questions. In addition, you enjoy the[4] fellowship of a congenial group of people.

A trailer tour also has the advantage that expenses are greatly[5] reduced, for you do not have any lodging costs and are able to do your own cooking.

Why not send for our[6] free booklet, *Touring America by Trailer*. It describes how you, too, can enjoy the pleasures of a trailer[7] tour. Yours very truly,   [144]

667 Dear Mr. Russell: Are you looking for a vacation that will be relaxing and unhurried, one in which you[1] can truly "get away from it all"? You can have this type of vacation if you take one of our cruises on our[2] ocean liner, the "John Hancock."

This lovely ship has all the modern facilities you would expect in a fine[3] hotel. You travel in an air-conditioned stateroom. A social hostess provides a program of entertainment[4] that will make every minute of your cruise an enjoyable one.

Seven cruises are planned for this year. Each one features[5] guided tours in many of the cities in the islands of the Pacific. Choose the cruise that appeals to you[6] most and make your reservation today. A 10 percent deposit now will hold your reservation until a[7] month before the departure date. Very truly yours, [150]

668 Gentlemen: My vacation this year is scheduled for the month of May, and my family and I are planning a[1] month's trip to Europe. We want to visit Norway, Denmark, and Sweden in May, at which time we understand that the[2] weather is usually fair in those countries.

I have been told that your agency specializes in arranging[3] guided tours to Europe. If you are conducting any tours in May that would include the countries of[4] Scandinavia, I would appreciate receiving information about them.

I am especially interested[5] in the following:
1. The complete itinerary
2. Lodging accommodations
3. The tourist-class[6] air fare

I am also interested in knowing whether your agency provides any type of financing plan[7] for payment over a period of time. Sincerely yours, [151]

669 Dear Mr. Kane: Thank you for your letter of April 20 inquiring about our all-expense trip on the[1] Fox Bus Line from Cincinnati to the Kentucky Derby.

The buses will leave the depot at South and Green Streets[2] at 8 a.m. on Saturday, May 6. The cost will be $60, which includes all taxes and tips. The trip[3] offers the following accommodations:
1. Transportation on our modern buses
2. A complete, delicious[4] box lunch
3. An excellent reserved seat at the track
4. Dinner at Louisville's famous Smith Hotel

If you[5] would like to enjoy a delightful day at the Kentucky Derby, make your reservations now. Cordially yours,[6] [120]

670 Dear Miss Tucker: Thank you for your letter of March 10 requesting information about our tours to Europe. We[1] are *delighted°* to provide the necessary travel accommodations for your group of 40 students from[2] Hartford College.

The enclosed folder describes our various European tours that are available this summer.[3] The first tour is scheduled to leave New York on Monday, June 10. The trip from New York to London will be on the[4] "Martha Washington," which accommodates 850 passengers. The folder also gives the itinerary,[5] which includes England, France, and Germany.

When your final plans are made, we hope that you will let us have the[6] *opportunity†* of completing the arrangements for your summer tour. Yours very truly, [137]

Also correct:
°glad, pleased
†privilege

LESSON 78

674 Dear Mr. Day: Thank you for your invitation to speak at the conference in Chicago on Friday, August[1] 10. I wish it were possible for me to accept, for I have always enjoyed attending your annual meetings[2] in the past. Unfortunately, I must attend an emergency meeting of our company's board of[3] directors on that day.

If you do not have another speaker in mind, I suggest that you invite Mr. James C.[4] Baker, vice president of the Commercial Travelers Association. I have heard Mr. Baker speak many[5] times, and I am confident that your members would enjoy hearing him.

I hope you will extend a similar[6] invitation to me in the future. Very truly yours,   [131]

675 Dear Dan: Since you are away from campus this summer, I thought I would let you know that our canoeing club is holding[1] its annual before-school trip from September 3 to September 16. We will be going to Fox Lake[2] in Minnesota.

The distance we hope to traverse is about 80 miles. We plan to travel at the easy[3] pace of five to ten miles a day, which will give us plenty of time for fishing, swimming, and just relaxing.

Would you[4] be interested in going on this trip? Reservations must be made by August 2. If you decide to join[5] us, I will be glad to take your reservation and send you a complete list of the equipment you will need to[6] bring with you. Cordially yours,   [125]

676 Dear Fred: Thank you for writing me about the trip the canoeing club is planning from September 3 to September[1] 16. It sounds very interesting. I wish I could join you; I know I would enjoy the trip thoroughly.[2]

Unfortunately, however, I will not be free during the month of September. Several weeks ago I[3] promised to type my brother's thesis, which he is now writing. He says he has already completed the initial[4] draft and that the final draft will be ready for typing the first of September. I estimate that it will[5] take me about two weeks to complete the typing.

I appreciate your thoughtfulness in writing me, and I hope[6] that you and the other members of the canoeing club have a delightful, enjoyable time. Sincerely yours,[7]   [140]

677 Dear Mr. Brown: The International Travel Agency is adding a new feature to the tours that we sponsor[1] for foreign visitors. We call the new program the Home Visit Plan. Under this plan, tourists from European[2] countries will visit American families in their homes for an afternoon or an evening. We feel[3] that this will be an interesting and beneficial experience for both visitors and hosts. The visitors[4] will be able to see what life in an American home is actually like, and the hosts will gain new[5] friends and new interests.

Our agency reimburses the hosting family for the cost of refreshments and[6] other incidental expenses. We feel the real benefit will be the enjoyment derived from meeting and[7] getting to know interesting, cultured people from other countries.

If you would like to be host to a foreign[8] visitor, please let us know. One of our representatives will call on you at your convenience to give you all[9] the essential details. You will not be placed under any obligation by his visit, Mr. Brown. Very[10] truly yours,   [201]

678 Dear Mr. Sands: We were happy to receive your letter of January 10 in which you accept our invitation[1] to visit our plant. We will have one of our employees meet Flight 211 on January 21[2] and drive you to the plant.

We have made arrangements for you to tour the plant and to meet with the superintendent.[3]

If you have not yet made reservations at a hotel in Seattle, may I suggest that you stay at the[4] Holiday Hotel, which is located about five blocks from the plant. Yours very truly,   [96]

679 Dear Mr. Jones: Would you like to stretch out and relax on your next trip from New York to Washington? Then take a[1] National bus.

With the new seating arrangement on our buses, you have plenty of leg room. A National bus will[2] get you to Washington in less than four hours for only $11 or $20 round trip. This[3] represents a saving of $16 over rail transportation and $32 over air shuttle[4] service.

So the next time business or pleasure takes you to Washington, take a National bus and stretch out and[5]

save. Yours truly,   [103]

680 Dear Mr. Abbey: I am impressed with the plan under which foreigners visiting the United States will spend some[1] time with American families. I discussed your offer with my wife and children, and they feel that nothing would[2] be nicer than to have these *visitors*° spend an evening with us.

The best time for us to act as hosts would be on[3] September 18, 19, or 20. If you can arrange a social visit on one of those evenings, please[4] let us know.

It will be a pleasure to take the visitors to dinner as our guests. We will be more than repaid[5] for our efforts by the pleasure that entertaining them will give us. Yours very truly,   [116]

Also correct:
°people, foreigners, folks

LESSON 79

684 Gentlemen: My family and I have arranged to take a three-week vacation together this year. As we have[1] heard that Canada is beautiful in the summer, we have decided to spend our vacation there. We plan to[2] visit Ottawa, Halifax, and a number of intermediate points.

We were told by a friend that you provide[3] a service of sending maps and other information to travelers to Canada. We would appreciate[4] it, therefore, if you would send us maps indicating the points of interest in eastern Canada and a[5] directory of hotels and motels. Sincerely yours,   [110]

685 Dear Mr. Block: We are happy to learn that you are planning to spend your vacation in Canada this year. We[1] are confident that you will enjoy Canada's lakes, forests, and other recreational facilities.

Enclosed[2] is a map of the area you plan to visit. We are also sending you separately a directory[3] of the hotels, motels, and other facilities that will be of interest to you.

Because eastern[4] Canada is a popular vacation spot for thousands of persons during the summer, you would be wise to make[5] your reservations early.

Best wishes, Mr. Block, for a pleasant, enjoyable vacation. Sincerely yours,[6]   [120]

686 Gentlemen: This letter has two purposes:

1. To tell you how much I have enjoyed your magazine, *Travel[1] Horizons*, during the years that I have been a subscriber.

2. To point out an error in the article entitled[2] "Shopping Tips," which appears in the April issue.

In the article the author says, "Although it is not[3] generally known by travelers abroad, it is legal to declare the wholesale value of merchandise purchased[4] overseas rather than the retail value." This statement was true under the law that was in effect several[5] years ago. However, the law was recently amended, and the traveler must now declare the actual[6] price that he paid for each item that he brings into this country.

In view of the possible burdens your readers[7] may be subjected to if they use wholesale prices in their declarations as a result of reading your article,[8] you might consider the advisability of running a short item in your June issue announcing[9] the change in the law. Very truly yours,   [187]

687 Dear Mr. Smith: Thank you for your kind invitation to visit your manufacturing plant in Seattle on[1] Friday, January 21. I will be arriving in Seattle on Western Airlines Flight 211[2] at the International Airport at 2 p.m. on that day.

Would it be possible for someone to meet me[3] at the air terminal and drive me to the plant?

I understand that the plant is located only a few miles[4] from the air terminal. If it is not convenient to have someone meet me, I will plan to take a taxi to[5] the plant. Cordially yours,   [104]

688 Dear Mr. McNair: You have been referred to us by the Southern Employment Agency as a possible candidate[1] for a position with our travel agency.

We are a large, nationally known travel agency[2] with *offices** in most of the major cities of the United States.

We have an opening at the present[3] time for a person with a successful record of supervising international travel tours.

If you would[4] like a position of responsibility with our organization, please fill out and return the enclosed[5] application form. If we find that you have the qualifications for the position, we will arrange for an[6] interview in our headquarters in Dal-

las. Sincerely yours, [131]
Also correct:
°branches

Office-Style Dictation

689 (*First letter, as dictated*) Dear Fred: As you will recall, last April I told you about my plans to spend two weeks in St. Croix at the Lake View Guest House which had been suggested to me by one of my associates. The Lake View Guest House serves no meals; it gives you an opportunity to eat at different places every day.

It was one of the best vacations I have ever had. This guest house is right on the water, and there is a private beach in front. [Put these last two sentences right after *by one of my associates.*]

I am sure that you and Grace would enjoy staying there—and the cost of the rooms is very reasonable. If you want more information, call me. Sincerely yours,

689 (*First letter, as it would be transcribed*) Dear Fred: As you will recall, last April I told you about my plans to spend two weeks in St. Croix at the Lake View[1] Guest House which had been suggested to me by one of my associates. It was one of the best vacations I[2] have ever had. This guest house is right on the water, and there is a private beach in front. The Lake View Guest House serves[3] no meals; it gives you an opportunity to eat at different places every day.

I am sure that you and[4] Grace would enjoy staying there—and the cost of the rooms is very reasonable.

If you want more information,[5] call me. Sincerely yours, [104]

689 (*Second letter, as dictated*) Dear Mr. Day: I sincerely appreciate your invitation to attend your conference in Detroit on June 15. I wish I could accept as I always enjoy your conferences.

My family has other plans for me, however. My family has decided that we should take a leisurely automobile trip to the West Coast. Two of my children will go away to school in the fall, and this summer will probably be the last that we can all vacation together. [Move the sentence beginning *my family has decided* down to this point.]

Thanks for your invitation. I know your conference will be a success as usual. Sincerely yours,

689 (*Second letter, as it would be transcribed*) Dear Mr. Day: I sincerely appreciate your invitation to attend your conference in Detroit on[1] June 15. I wish I could accept as I always enjoy your conferences.

My family has other plans[2] for me, however. Two of my children will go away to school in the fall, and this summer will probably be[3] the last that we can all vacation together. My family has decided that we should take a leisurely[4] automobile trip to the West Coast.

Thanks for your invitation. I know your conference will be a success as[5] usual. Sincerely yours, [105]

LESSON 80

692   *Travel Know-How*

Practical know-how is acquired in the hard school of experience, and the field of international travel[1] is no exception to this rule. Fortunately, with so much information available on the subject, there[2] is little or no excuse for ignorance of basic travel requirements.

All international carriers[3] publish advice on every phase of travel. Travel agencies are loaded with recommendations designed[4] to reduce wear and tear on the traveler as well as to save time and money.

It is difficult to package[5] travel know-how to meet individual requirements, but here are some recommendations of a general nature[6] that can make the difference between success and failure of an overseas trip:

1. Plan your travel sufficiently[7] in advance to give yourself time to learn something about the countries you intend to visit. Get some background[8] on their history, culture, customs, scenic areas, and native foods.

Travel agents and transportation[9] companies have an abundance of helpful literature of this type. The embassies and consular offices[10] of foreign countries also provide informative brochures highlighting the attractions of their countries.

2.[11] Don't try to cover too much ground on one trip. It is better to cover less territory and see it well enough[12] to retain clear and happy memories than to see too much and return with only a blurred impression.

3.[13] Try to learn some basic words and phrases in one or more foreign languages; they work like magic. But if this is[14] impossible, remember that most people respond to a smile and will try to help you regardless of the language[15] barrier. Always remember that it is up to you to make the necessary adjustment to the customs[16] observed in the countries you visit.

4. Your passport should be valid for at least the length of your trip overseas,[17] and your visas should be in order. Your international certificate of vaccination should be up[18] to date. You should inquire into the baggage allowances for tourist and first-class travel. Before you make your[19] trip, you should learn the customs regulations of the United States as well as those of the countries you plan to[20] visit.

5. Don't burden yourself with excess baggage. Unless you are going to a particularly remote[21] corner of the world, you will find essentials such as soap, towels, medicines, and cosmetics available[22] everywhere.

Don't overdress and don't underdress. Select your wardrobe carefully and in keeping with the climate[23] and temperature to which you will be subjected.

6. Don't load yourself down with useless souvenirs and tourist trinkets.[24] If you want a memento, buy something you will enjoy seeing and using for some time to come.

7. Watch your[25] diet. Enjoy the food specialties of the countries you visit, but apply common sense to

your eating habits.[26] Don't overtire yourself; travel is more strenuous than you think, and it is no fun being ill away from home.[27]

8. Keep your sense of humor. Your best-made plans can go wrong. There is an element of human error that you must[28] be ready to cope with no matter where you are. Getting angry at other people won't solve whatever difficulty[29] you may be in.

9. When you need information or guidance, go to a reputable source for assistance.[30] If you wish to hire a car, for example, go to a reliable agency, which will arrange for all the[31] permits, documents, and insurance you require.

If you are in any kind of difficulty or need information[32] or advice of an official nature, remember that the United States embassy or consulate[33] is your home away from home. [666]

693 Dear Mr. Smith: When you fly to Japan on our Flight 115, you will get more than a choice of entrees; you will[1] get a choice of menus. This is true in both first class and in economy class.

One menu features a complete[2] Japanese dinner consisting of the same dishes that the Japanese serve their honored guests in their homes. The other[3] features a continental dinner in which you have a choice of several international delicacies.[4]

Whichever you choose, you will enjoy the courteous, thoughtful service you will receive from our staff. The next time[5] you fly to Japan, specify our Flight 115. It will be an experience you will never forget. Cordially[6] yours, [122]

694 Dear Mr. Smith: The wise traveler never makes a business trip without consulting the Johnson *Travel Directory*,[1] that tells all about the 450 Johnson Motor Inns that we operate. It lists their rates, their[2] accommodations, and their recreational facilities. It even has maps that will guide you to the Johnson[3] Motor Inn you have chosen once you arrive in town.

No matter where you are going or how you are getting[4] there, we promise you that this little book will make your trip more comfortable.

To get your copy of the Johnson[5] *Travel Directory*, request one on your business letterhead. If you prefer, call us at (600)[6] 211-5556. That is our toll-free, 24-hour reservation number.

While you are at it, request complete[7] data about our guaranteed rates for businessmen. Cordially yours, [153]

Appendix

RECALL DRILLS

Joined Word Endings

1 Treatment, alignment, supplement, amusement.

2 Nation, termination, station, operation, inflation.

3 Credential, confidential, essential, commercial, socially.

4 Greatly, namely, nicely, mainly, nearly.

5 Readily, speedily, easily, hastily, necessarily, family.

6 Careful, thoughtful, delightful, mindful, usefulness.

7 Assume, assumption, resume, resumption, presume, presumption, consumer, consumed.

8 Dependable, reliable, profitable, table, troubled.

9 Gather, gathered, together, rather, either, leather, bother, bothered, neither.

10 Actual, actually, gradual, schedule, annual, equally.

11 Furniture, picture, nature, stature, captured, miniature, failure, natural.

12 Yourself, myself, itself, himself, herself, themselves, ourselves, yourselves.

13 Port, sport, import, report, deportment.

14 Contain, retain, certain, container, contained.

15 Efficient, sufficient, deficient, efficiency, deficiency, proficiency.

Disjoined Word Endings

16 Childhood, motherhood, neighborhood, brotherhood.

17 Forward, backward, onward, afterward, rewarded.

18 Relationship, steamship, authorship, professorship, championship.

19 Radical, technical, political, article, chemically, periodically, logically.

20 Congratulate, regulate, stipulates, tabulated, congratulation, regulation, regulations, stipulations.

21 Willingly, exceedingly, knowingly, surprisingly, grudgingly.

22 Readings, mornings, sidings, dressings, savings, drawings, sayings, blessings, feelings.

23 Program, telegram, diagrams.

24 Notification, modification, specifications, classifications.

25 Personality, ability, reliability, facilities, utility, generalities.

26 Faculty, penalty, casualty.

27 Authority, sincerity, majority, minority, clarity, sorority, charity, seniority.

Joined Word Beginnings

28 Permit, perform, perfect, pertain, persist, purchase, pursue, pursued, purple, purse.

29 Employ, empower, embarrass, embody, empire, emphatic, embrace, emphasis.

30 Impress, impression, imply, impossible, impair, impel, imbue, impact.

31 Increase, intend, income, inform, inconsistent, indeed, inference, inferior.

32 Enlarge, enforce, enlist, encourage, encounter, encircle, enrich, enrage.

33 Unkind, unwritten, unwilling, unsuccessful, undo, unpleasant, untie, unpopular.

34 Refer, resign, receive, reform, reorganize.

35 Beneath, believe, belong, before, became.

36 Delay, deliver, deserve, diligent.

37 Dismiss, disappoint, discover, discuss, despite.

38 Mistake, misquote, misspell, misstate, misunderstand, misapplied, mistrust.

39 Explain, excite, extend, excuse, express.

40 Comprise, comfort, comply, completed.

41 Condition, consult, continue, confident, convey, confess.

42 Submit, substantiate, subdivide, sublease, suburban.

43 Almost, also, already, although, alteration.

44 Forget, forceful, performed, forecast, foreman.

45 Furnish, furnished, furnishings, furniture, furnace, further.

46 Turn, turned, term, attorney, determine.

47 Ultimate, ulterior, adult, culture, result.

Disjoined Word Beginnings

48 Postman, postage, postmaster, postponed, post office.

49 Interested, internal, interview, intercept, introduce, introduction, enterprise, entrances, entertain, entered.

50 Electricity, electrician, electrical, electric wire, electric fan, electric light, electric motor.

51 Supervise, supervision, supervisor, superhuman, superb.

52 Circumstance, circumstances, circumstantial, circumvent, circumspect.

53 Selfish, self-made, self-defense, self-respect, self-conscious.

54 Transit, transfer, transact, transplant, translation.

55 Understand, undertake, undergo, underpaid, undermine.

56 Overcome, overdue, overhead, overture, overpay, oversee.

Phrase Drills

57 To see, to sell, to put, to place, to begin, to have, to be, to fly, to fit, to share, to which.

58 Had been, have been, I have been, have not been, has been, has not been, it has been, you should have been, you might have been, I could have been, he would have been.

59 To be able, would be able, had been able, has been able, have not been able, I have not been able, you would be able, should be able, I could be able, you should be able, I will be able.

60 I want, you want, they want, we want, she wants, who wants, if you want, do you want, if you wanted, they wanted, I wanted.

61 Days ago, weeks ago, months ago, years ago, few days ago, some time ago.

62 Able to say, able to see, glad to see, in order to be, in order to be

able, in order to have, in addition to the, in addition to this.

63 During the past, in the past, in the future, during the year, during the last, in the world, on the question, about the matter, by the way, on the part, on the subject, upon the subject.

64 Many of the, many of these, many of them, out of date, out of this, out of the, one of the, one of them, some of our, some of these, some of them, none of the, none of them.

65 At a loss, as a result, for a few days, for a few minutes, for a few months, for a long time, for a moment, in a position, in a few days, in a few months, in such a way.

66 a.m., p.m., C.O.D., Chamber of Commerce, vice versa.

67 Of course, of course it is, as soon as, as soon as possible, to do, I hope, we hope, to us, let us, let us know, your order, to me, to make, to know, Dear Mr., Dear Mrs., Dear Madam, Dear Sir, Yours sincerely, Sincerely yours, Very sincerely, Yours respectfully, Respectfully yours, Very truly, Very truly yours, Yours very truly, Cordially yours, Very cordially yours.

KEY TO CHARTS ON INSIDE BACK COVER

Frequently Used Phrases of Gregg Shorthand

1 Of the, in the, to the, we are, for the, on the, it is.

2 To you, we have, will be, of your, of our, that the, with the.

3 I am, and the, at the, to be, of this, you can, I have.

4 You have, you are, by the, to make, from the, for you, there is.

5 In our, is the, that is, we can, in this, to have, to get.

6 For your, so that, of course, on your, they are, there are, have been.

7 To see, we shall, to us, you may, about the, we will, may be.

8 One of our, with you, one of the, should be, to do, would be, to me.

9 If you, as the, very much, you will, with us, and that, you will find.

10 He is, on our, it will, of these, will you please, any other, I am sure.

11 Can be, for this, in which, to take, we shall be glad, for our, if the.

12 To give, with our, from you, I shall, is not, that will, I was.

13 Not only, to know, through the, has been, I think, if you will, when the.

14 For us, this is, to buy, as soon as, you will be, to keep, we should.

15 Do not, I know, it will be, that this, to pay, we may, it was.

16 That are, we know, if you have, what is, they have, in his, of his.

17 As you, in order, to come, as well, does not, you know, you need.

18 At least, if you are, on this, sending you, some of the, we have been, we want.

19 He was, hear from you, you want, into the, must be, send us, Sincerely yours.

*Brief Forms of Gregg
Shorthand in Alphabetical
Order*

1 A-an, about, acknowledge, advantage, advertise, after, am.

2 And, are-our-hour, at-it, be-by, between, big, business.

3 But, can, character, characters, circular, company, correspond-correspondence.

4 Could, difficult, during, enclose, envelope, ever-every, experience.

5 For, from, general, gentlemen, glad, gone, good.

6 Govern, government, great, have, his-is, how-out, I.

7 Idea, immediate, importance-important, in-not, manufacture, merchandise, merchant.

8 Morning, Mr., Mrs., must, never, newspaper, next.

9 Object, objected, of, one (won), opinion, opportunity, order.

10 Ordinary, organize, over, part, particular, present, probable.

11 Progress, public, publication-publish, purpose, put, quantity, question.

12 Railroad, railroads, recognize, regard, regular, request, responsible.

13 Satisfactory-satisfy, send, several, shall, short, should, situation.

14 Soon, speak, state, street, subject, success, such.

15 Suggest, than, thank, that, the, there (their), them.

16 They, thing-think, this, those, throughout, time, under.

17 Upon, use, value, very, was, well-will, were-year.

18 What, when, where, which, why, wish, with.

19 Work, world, worth, would, yesterday, yet, you-your.